WHERE'S MY DOG? THE SEARCH S

What a bizarre title. But it is interesting, isn't it? Doesn't it make you ask, *"What could this be all about"?* Well, the truth is, it's not about dogs at all; it's about leadership and honesty.

Nevertheless, dogs are a useful metaphor. You see, dogs are the closest thing we can find when searching for examples of uncompromising honesty. Dishonesty is not part of their DNA. In contrast, the problem for many leaders today is that at some level "most people lie".

This may seem like a provocative statement but it's true, even though most of the time we do not even know we are doing it. Some, including many renowned psychologists, would even say that at some level we need to lie to survive. *Do we?*

In a world of business, sports and political Watergates and scandals that has even culminated in Papal resignations against a background of "vatileaks", we seem to suffer from a paradoxical scenario. We find ourselves contrasting the lack of honesty that brought down many of our business and sporting figures as exemplified by the likes of Madoff, Lance Armstrong and Oscar Pistorius (to name a few), with the apparent total honesty of leaders such as the Dalai Lama, Kofi Anan and even Richard Branson or Steve Jobs.

We all know that whilst some leaders command respect, others do not. Some leaders have willing followers, whilst others are followed through coercion. Some may lose their followers, whilst others should never have any. And some allow their egos to block trust, whilst others are dealers in trust.

This book is therefore a journey into one of the hottest topics for leaders today – **honest leadership**. It sniffs and scratches around the undergrowth searching for the real meaning of honesty and leadership and finishes up helping you uncover your own truth. And with the aid of a remarkably simple idea – the Eight Axioms of Honest Leadership – this book will provide you with the tools and skills to enable you to identify, train and maybe even tame your own leadership approach and help you to become a "top dog".

For information, address all queries to:

WM Consulting, Weidhofmatt 8, CH – 6044 Udligenswil

info@honest-leader.com
www.honest-leader.com

FIRST EDITION

ISBN 978-3-033-03950-6

WHERE'S MY DOG?

THE SEARCH FOR HONEST LEADERSHIP.

BY

DAVID. B. WATKINS

"Most of what I say is complete truth. My edit button is broken."
– Myra McEntire, author "Hourglass"

"If a dog will not come to you after having looked you in the face, you should go home and examine your conscience."
– Woodrow Wilson US President 1913 – 1921

For Lucretia & Gareth

- *MY* HONEST LEADERS

Contents

THE THANKS BIT

Read me! I start with this part as it is important that you read it. Every book seems to have one of these sections and it almost always appears to be stuffed in as an acknowledgement in the closing pages. It becomes forgotten, in the same way that a child discards an unwanted gift at Christmas. And, let's be honest, how many of us read these parts? Do we really care what's in it? I mean, it's just the author extending their eulogies to a bunch of people we do not know, never meet and frankly probably do not care about! It doesn't change the book does it?

But this book is about "honesty", which implies "good" and "bad", and "right" and "wrong". So what's wrong with saying "thanks" at the beginning? And what's wrong with you understanding why I am saying thanks and to whom? After all, most books you ever read are <u>never</u> the result of only one person's work.

And anyway, "thanks" seems to be the right thing to do, especially if you have got partners who stand by you, other contributors who have inspired you or friends and colleagues who have coached, badgered or annoyed you during the writing process. All these people are necessary.

First and foremost my family for accepting that the only conversation they received from me for a few months was a meaningless diatribe of book related content that they could not place into context until they had seen the first, presumably semi-sensible draft.

Also a huge debt of gratitude to all those who have taken time to put their "fingers to the keyboard" and share their perspectives, stories and experiences about honesty and honest leadership. In alphabetical order: David Barker, Trix Heberlein, Daniel Huber and Helene Leimer. Also to Alex Woollham for your illustrative expertise. You all make the book special and I thank you. Thanks also to the feedback and thought provoking conversations with Sabina, Gareth and Lindsay each of whom have helped me fine tune the content; and finally to Lucretia for her detailed eyes, editorial skill and help in getting me to shape the content to be fit for print.

I also want to thank the guys and gals who fill the internet with content. OMG! I have no clue how long it would have taken me sitting alone in dusty basements of city libraries, hunting through back issues of yellowed newspapers and reading oddball magazines in the search for useful guidance for my pages. I presume I would have never finished and this pet project would have died a death in the grey cells of my mind.

This book is dedicated to two special people. First my wife Lucretia, without whose unwavering support and guidance I would not be able to do the things I want or explore the paths I feel I must. She is my driving force, a true and (mostly) silent, loyal and honest leader working behind the scenes. She has a favourite motto that every so often I am reminded of: "Behind every successful man stands a women telling him what to do". Maybe, just maybe, she is sometimes right.

Second to Gareth, an honest leader, coach, guru and dear friend whose values and beliefs have enabled me to question myself, mature (well sometimes) where I needed to grow and help me in my endeavours to get my personal star to shine at the right time, for the right reasons and at the right intensity. If you ever write your book(s), I am sure they will be a gem.

I hope this book is all that you both expected.

THE POINT OF THIS BOOK

This is not a book about searching for dogs. That's the truth. It is a book about leadership and honesty. But I am assuming that you are also intrigued by the rather bizarre title. It makes you want to dig a little deeper and learn more doesn't it?

Let me explain – I believe that dogs are the closest things that humans can relate to when searching for examples of uncompromising honesty. They simply cannot lie. Therefore I use "honest dogs" as a metaphor throughout the book.

For those amongst you who own dogs, more often than not you may have noticed it's your dog that greets you first when you come home – not your kids, or your partner – but your hairy, smelly dog.

> "Some leaders command respect, others do not. Some leaders have willing followers, whilst others are followed through coercion. Some leaders have lost their followers, and some will never have any hope of getting any"

It does not know if you have had a bad day. But it's always there saying hello, isn't it? It does not understand that you feel all grumbly when you have to clean up after it. But as long as you are nice, it wags its whole body and appears delighted that it may show its loyalty with a big wet friendly lick.

But we also know that not all dogs are perfect. When they are untrained and over eager they become impatient and uncomfortable to take on a walk. They pull at the line, dragging you into bushes and other places you do not want to go. They leave their mess, do not respond to our orders and whistles or simply run off towards a single-minded target leaving us standing helpless and dogless. "Where's my dog?" we must ask.

Dogs have personalities and just like humans will react differently in different situations. Some are demure, others aggressive. Some lead, others follow. Some are the natural king of the pack, others meek and introvert. Some intelligent and cunning, others just plain dumb. And that I believe is exactly the same with leaders and their followers.

Some leaders command respect, others do not. Some leaders have willing followers, whilst others are followed through coercion. Some leaders have lost their followers and some will never have any hope of getting any. And this is the point of the metaphor and our search for honesty. Dogs follow when owners are honest. And we are no different with our leaders – be they politicians we have voted for, sports heroes we idolise or our boss we work for. We are not searching for a lost dog, but rather for our honest leader, our "top dog".

The only problem is we all lie. I know that is a provocative statement but it is true, even though most of the time we do not know we are doing it or we are able to easily justify it. But as you will see, some psychologists even argue that we need to lie to survive! But do we?

This book is intended to provoke debate and thought. Not about dogs of course, but about honest leadership. It is aimed at individuals and executives who may have some leadership experience and who are interested in taking a timely subject and discussing it with others in the bar, around a camp fire, over the water cooler, in the board room, or in a vets waiting lounge. Important is that at the end, you draw your own conclusions about the subject at hand.

The book takes a light-hearted look into honesty and leadership, understanding what we mean by "honest" and "leadership" and debating why all this is important anyway. It will help you identify, train and perhaps tame your own honest leadership approach. It will help you to become a "top dog". If this appeals, read it.

I hope that in reading the book, you consider what honest leadership means to yourself. How do you view the subject? What does it mean for you in your interactions with others? Do your means justify the end? Do you want or need to change? Do you want to be a top dog? How do your followers view you?

My words may make you angry, or make you laugh or even at times make you uncomfortable. You may even as a result throw the book into the nearest wastepaper bin or delete it out of your portable reader. Either way, if it makes you think about the issues I raise, then I consider that the book has succeeded in its task. Enjoy!

THE JOURNEY WE WILL TAKE

"A dog is one of the remaining reasons why some people can be persuaded to go for a walk."

– O.A. Battista, Canadian chemist & author

Every good dog walk has a destination in mind, but is ultimately a circuitous route back home. In our case home is the last page of the book, and once there, you will be able to gather your thoughts and make some decisions.

But getting home implies we must first embark on a journey. You will be guided on a thoughtful loop through six different parts. These will include getting to grips with a common understanding of what honesty actually is, how this knowledge will reap benefits when combined with great leadership and of course how to take the initial steps to being more honest. Our walk may take a couple of diversions as we proceed, and like any good dog, we may dump our thoughts or sniff out other content from more interesting places.

But whatever you choose when you do get home, I recommend that you do not take off your lead, take a drink from the water bowl and search out a nice place to lie down. Rather you should start your search for your own honesty and in doing that become a top dog. Honesty begins and ends with you; not your partners, kids, boss, priest or your dog. Ultimately you are the one with the power to be that top (honest) dog. It is you who should walk the right walk, and bark the right bark.

Throughout the book we will also take a look at some well-known leaders and organisations and try to judge whether or not they are honest. They may help you form an opinion, provide a sanity check or just simply offer inspiration. There are many leaders and companies I could have selected, but those I have chosen are I believe the most fascinating.

The style and tonality I have used is not intended to create complexity or over simplify the issue. Saying that, it should be simple and easy to read, some might even say it is entertaining. I do however knowingly take some elements out of context and therefore many of you may find yourself out of your comfort zone. I may make you squirm but it should not be offensive, rather to provoke thought – you will know what I am referring to when you get there.

For good measure, I also decided to throw in a few theoretical models and related research that I stumbled across. I do not pretend to be a trained psychologist and so I freely use my own opinion and certainly a touch of bias in the interpretation of this research if I believe it adds value to the point I am making. All outside input is referred to in the "further searching" pages at the back of this book.

Finally, our journey will conclude with a model and some guidance that will help you start your personal journey towards honest leadership. Do with this as you will – but do at least think about it.

PART I
SEARCHING FOR HONESTY

"It is discouraging how many people are shocked by honesty and how few by deceit."
– Noel Coward, Playwright and composer 1899 – 1973

"Oh, what a tangled web we weave... when first we practice to deceive."
– Walter Scott, Playwright and Novelist 1771 – 1832

"If your dog doesn't like someone you probably shouldn't either."
– Unknown

Every day most people lie. We probably do not intend to start the day planning to hide the truth from our families, friends and colleagues but in reality that's how many of us go through our waking hours. We probably could not survive without it. We do it to protect firstly ourselves and secondly our loved ones. Mostly we do not even know we are doing it.

It starts with an innocent enough question – "*how are you*?", but if you think about it, this question is already loaded and setting you up for your first lie of the day. Especially when we answer with "*not bad*" or "*fine thanks*", or even if we ask the same in return and pretend as if it *really* matters.

Clearly, we do not tell the truth when faced with this kind of question. We use our edit button when we answer. Even if we really are fine, we still keep something back. We start our day by lying! And we do not even think about it. It's habit! This is our honest day.

Is this how Bernhard Madoff started his days before deciding to swindle billions of dollars out of his customers, or Osama Bin Laden before he decided to order the world's largest terrorist attack? Is this how Barack Obama starts his day before deciding on the fate of a bill that could impact the entire US economy? Or how Steve Jobs started his days before going out to inspire millions with his next creation? By lying? That can't be right, can it?

The fact is, honesty is a fundamental basis to the functioning of human society. Our interpretation of it, our need for it, our avoidance of it or simply our playing at it helps us determine our actions, our decisions and our interactions with others. Our decision to be honest or not will determine how others judge us. It is ultimately our legacy. It's the one thing that we leave behind that people will remember us for – positively or negatively.

This first part is about laying the scent and getting our dog primed to search the undergrowth for honesty. We will sniff it out, and in doing so understand what honesty is, what it probably isn't, whether or not we are good at it, and finally whether a lack or abundance of it has anything to do with our intelligence.

HONESTY IS THE BEST POLICY. OR IS IT?

As a kid my parents always told me that lying was bad and being honest was good. But somehow I found this rather confusing. On the one hand if I had done something wrong and owned up to it, my parents praised me for my honesty. But on the other hand I still got punished for the bad deed I had done in the first place. So how does that work then? Being punished for being honest? Surely there is something wrong with the picture here? Where was my incentive for being honest – in my teenage mind it was hardly the best policy.

Similarly, do you really think that being honest is best if you send someone into an anorexic spiral because you told them they looked fat and should lose a few kilos? Is it better to conceal your real thoughts? Is it even better to lie?

I think this proverb has a frustratingly "feel good" factor to it, for it simply infers that we should conduct our lives in perfect honesty. But I am sure you agree that this does not really happen. No-one is perfectly honest. Are we? When was the last time you lied? Or put another way, when did you last not tell the "whole" truth or did you allow a tiny fib to fall out of your mouth? Ask yourself if you still believe in Santa? I presume you do not, but do you tell your kids the truth or let them believe the magic until they figure it out for themselves?

Back in 2000 an article in Time Magazine, "Deceitful Lies" quoted David Nyberg a philosophy professor at the University of New York as saying, *"Truth telling is morally overrated,"* ...."*Being against all deception is as wrong-minded as loathing all bacteria-including the ones responsible for wine and cheese. A lifetime of relationships is inconceivable without deception".*

Peter Stiegnitz, social psychologist at the University of Budapest, argues that most lying is simply undertaken to avoid trouble. His studies in the past have shown that 41% of lies are to conceal misbehaviour ("I was working late last night"), while another 14% are the little white lies that make social life possible ("I'd love to come to dinner, but I've got a prior commitment that evening"). The rest, Stiegnitz says, have to do with everything from us wanting to be loved through to sheer laziness. Fortunately our lies are in most cases relatively harmless.

But what about those occasions when it seems OK to lie? Can you have "good" lies? And have you ever considered those amongst us who will be honest only if it pays off, and even knowingly dishonest if they think this will pay off more? Can you trust anyone? I am sure you will immediately say "yes of course, my husband/wife/partner". But how do you know they do not lie to you? Even to protect your feelings?

There is no rarity to lying. It happens nearly every day – in the newspapers, in politics, in annual corporate reports and you may even lie to yourself. We lie all the time, either to protect ourselves, protect others or just out of plain habit and we often do so without even thinking. It may be a simple distortion of the truth a little white lie or omission of facts – but we all do it. Don't we? Deception to a great or lesser extent has become part of our everyday lives.

Nietzsche, a German philosopher alive around 150 years ago, believed that "lying is a necessity of life". Stiegnitz believes that telling falsehoods are "an essential part of survival in everyday life" and "as necessary to life as air and water". Nyberg also believes that without lying, it would be virtually impossible to have a relationship. He states "To live decently with one another, we do not need moral purity, we need discretion… what does a child need before sleep – reality or comfort"? Society could not survive if we felt compelled to always tell the truth.

> "Telling falsehoods are an essential part of survival in everyday life and as necessary to life as air and water"

Is there a difference between men and women in this respect? Are men less stained by moral corruption than women? Well, Stiegnitz discovered that men lie on average 20% more than women – he also found that women are better liars than men, so arguably this does not make females more honest than males – rather more artful at deceit. And I am not sure this is a thing to be proud of! In the interest of maintaining a balanced perspective, let us also consider the reasons why men and women lie.

Catharina Lohmann, author of "women lie differently", argues that men lie mostly in relation to their careers – conversely women lie to protect their family and children. She states that "a man deceives for profit and egotism… he lies most cleverly and effectively at the levers of power". On the other hand *"women lie more readily [in social situations] than men because they are more sensitive"* she says.

But, male or female, how many lies can we handle? How many webs can we weave before we get caught out? And please do not say you don't lie. If you believe that, you are probably a liar, at least to yourself. A psychology study by Gerald Jellison found that the average person lies about 150 to 200 times per day. That means we are telling porkies almost every 5 – 10 minutes! So if this were true, what happened to "honesty is the best policy"? If we are lying every 5 minutes, do we even have time left to be honest?

I could therefore argue that being honest takes too much time and effort. That we are so busy being dishonest that any attempt to do otherwise will possibly not be appreciated or understood. We might therefore ask ourselves if being honest is even worth it – will it for example protect your career, help you win that big sale or cement your relationship? Does being honest really change anything we do or achieve?

A past boss once said to me *"you make me nervous by what you're not telling me…. I have the nagging doubt you always have something more going on behind the scenes"*. Now that is not necessarily lying, but could be argued that I was not being completely honest. But in this day and age does that make me a compulsive story teller or a smart cookie protecting myself from potential harm? If I was entirely honest, would I be treated differently or would I expose myself to risk as my future strategies become clear to others? In a business world, we are constantly playing games and we find ourselves working out the pros and cons of being completely honest.

But what do I even mean by honesty? In a time when political figures actively seek to hide the truth to protect against terrorism, and senior executives of global organisations appear to manipulate earnings reports for personal or organisational gain, is it at all surprising that we have perhaps lost track of what honesty actually is?

Even pop stars sing about the lack of honesty as they open their soul for all to hear. Billy Joel, in his soulful tune titled "Honesty" declares:

> *But if you look for truthfulness*
> *You might just as well be blind.*
> *It always seems to be so hard to give.*

> *Honesty is such a lonely word.*
> *Everyone is so untrue.*
> *Honesty is hardly ever heard*

So what is honesty? There are many similar definitions to be found, but I like to summarise honesty as *"truthfulness, sincerity or frankness"* which seems simple enough. Folk etymology proposes that "sincere" is derived from the Latin *"sine"* meaning *"without"* and *"cera",* meaning *"wax".* Allegedly, sculptors in Rome or Greece would cover flaws in their work with wax to deceive the viewer; therefore, a sculpture "without wax" (*"sinecera"*) would mean honesty in its perfection.

Today we clearly do not smother ourselves with wax to cover our flaws, but we are lying more than ever to get through the complexity of our daily lives. Therefore if we want to reach the end of this journey and consciously make an effort to become more honest, I believe we should also understand the "components", "traits", "drivers", "beliefs" or "morals" that make up honesty and try to consider how we may be able to "flex" these things in our everyday lives in order that we can become more self-aware of our actions. Stiegnitz said *"Be honest about lying... don't stop doing it, but acknowledge that you are doing it".*

THE TRUTH ABOUT TRUTH

On the face of it we may have thought that being honest should be pretty easy. Is it not a simple matter of telling the truth? Even Einstein once said *"whoever is careless with the truth in small matters cannot be trusted with the truth in big matters"*. Modern day writers, such as Virginia Woolf wrote *"If you cannot tell the truth about yourself, you cannot tell the truth about other people"*.

But is honesty as simple as being truthful? In fact I wonder, what is "the truth"? Is it the opposite of a lie? And if so, what is a lie? Is it concealing the truth? Or just partly concealing the truth? We have only just started to scratch the surface and already it's getting jolly confusing. Or is it simpler than it seems?

Historically, the old English and the Old High German origins of the word find itself rooted in concepts related to faith, honesty, sincerity, loyalty and agreement with fact and reality. Latin (Romance) languages relate to "veritas" or virtue whilst others such as Greek ("aletheia", meaning "unclosed") finds the meaning of truth in different etymological origins.

"Truth does not exist, as everyone's truth is theoretically different"

Today, the challenge to our understanding of "truth" starts when we begin to accept that "our truth" may not be the same as someone else's truth. Every day we are inundated with tons of information and data via the radio, TV, internet, email, blogs, social media, tweets etc. As a result we are consistently asking our brain to filter out what is necessary and what is not necessary for us to know.

The chances that you and I have the same background beliefs and subsequently filter the same information, from the same source, in the same way are very slim. This means that whatever you perceive as being "true" to you, maybe different to my perception of the truth. Understanding this fact is probably a great start to accepting that truth does not exist, as everyone's truth is theoretically different. So was Einstein wrong?

I do not think so, because the term "truth" has been the subject of debate in many circles. "Truth" is typically meant to refer to some fact or reality, or an orientation to a standard or an ideal. But for some scholars such a simplified approach is insufficient.

They might argue that it is important that we consider "truth" more deeply as it is an accepted, fundamental and very necessary component of everyday life. Let's be realistic – the human race conducts many of its economic, social, religious and political activities based on the concept that something or someone is "true" which therefore allows us to plan, prepare and evolve.

Truth, according to the Hindu religion and the ancient text of the Mahabharata (Santi Parva, Book 12, Section CLXII), is as follows "*Truth... as it exists in the entire world, is of thirteen kinds. The forms that Truth assumes are impartiality, self-control, forgiveness, modesty, endurance, goodness, renunciation, contemplation, dignity, fortitude, compassion, and abstention from injury. These... are the thirteen forms of Truth*" [although I count only 12...]. Further; "*truth is immutable, eternal, and unchangeable. It may be acquired through practices, which do not militate against any of the other virtues. It may also be acquired through Yoga*".

Assuming we do not wish to take up yoga in an effort to discover truth, let's look at other scholars and writers who have different perspectives. Many have moved beyond religion and attempt instead a philosophical approach to understanding truth. In the first century AD, Pontius Pilate (*John* 18:38) asked "*What is truth*?" but he received no answer. In the last century the concept and ideals of truth have been more deeply studied than at any previous time, and arguably some progress has been made.

One of the central aspects that many philosophers study has been the use of the word truth versus the opposite, "false". For example, when we say that London is South of the North Pole, the philosopher will contrast true with false rather than with "fake" or "insincere". After all, this is a factual statement. More generally, philosophers want to know what sorts of things are true and what sorts of things are false.

In researching these thoughts I had a small headache when I realised that the study of truth stretched across thousands of years and some 10 – 12 theories, some of which I found to be relatively easy to understand, yet others somewhat mathematical and quite ugly in their complexity. Not having a philosophy degree and bearing in mind these pages are only intended to help us understand a possible relationship between truth and honesty, I have chosen to briefly summarise the five generally accepted theories. If you find these interesting, you are encouraged to visit *Google* and do your own research.

Correspondence Theory: This stretches way back to the ancient Greek Philosophers such as Aristotle, and essentially states that true beliefs and statements correspond to an actual state of affairs. As the thirteenth century philosopher stated "*A judgment is said to be true when it conforms to the external reality*". In simple terms, it's only true if it's proven fact.

The supporters of this theory effectively state that truth is a matter of accurately copying objective reality and transferring this into thoughts, words, symbols etc. However, opponents of this theory argue that language [translation], culture, beliefs, attitudes and bias will not capture the full statement and can create an inaccurate interpretation.

Further, the way the sentence is written is also important. For example, stating, "I like chocolate" can depend very much on who "I" is. If it is written by David who likes chocolate, then it is true – conversely if it came from Bill who does not like chocolate, then it is false. Then we have a contradiction in the construction of the sentence which is not acceptable. It is not factually correct. The sentence or the proposition within the sentence (in this case, "liking chocolate") is the key to determining whether or not it is true.

Coherence Theory: This theory argues that a number of elements or propositions must align, support one another and be part of a complete system to be true, versus correspondence theory which requires only one element to be factually correct.

Constructivist Theory: This idea holds that truth is built over time and social progress, interspersed with the usual power and social struggles within a community. It argues that our perception of truth has been constructed based upon social experiences and human perception over time and this can stray from pure reality. Giambattista Vico, one such believer, argued that history and culture were man-made – *verum ipsum factum* – "*truth itself is constructed*". Marx is another example, who argued that political power can change ones perception of true knowledge and gained knowledge – and therefore our belief of truth and falsehood. In other words, bang the drum long enough and we start to believe it.

Consensus Theory: Believers of this theory argue that information becomes true when it is agreed upon by a group or sub group of people to generate consensus. I am sure there are many good and bad examples, but those that particularly stick in my mind are the ideals espoused by religious cults such as "The Church of Bible Understanding" (previously known as the Forever Family). This was started in the 1970's by Stuart Traill who believes he is the reincarnation of Elijah and claims he knows the date that Christ will reappear.

I do not wish to be the judge about Traill's predictions, but I do find it rather worrying that he has managed to persuade enough followers that his claim is the truth, such that many in this "group" have been members since their teens and devote up to 90% of their income to bringing Jesus back to life. Interestingly, Traill's personal wait for Jesus is suffered in supreme comfort whilst he enjoys the trappings of a half million dollar mansion and four aircraft.

Pragmatic Theory: There are a number of scholars behind this idea, that in essence states that truth is verified when someone puts their ideas into practice. One scholar, Charles Pierce, argues that theories such as the correspondence theory are only nominal truth – they do not become real truth until the concept is tested.

Whether or not you find your own truth in these theories is only something you can know. But do not worry if you are not sure – even the intelligent philosophers don't seem to always agree about what is truth.

I rather believe the bigger challenge lies not in our understanding of what truth is, but rather accepting that truth appears intuitively to be quite hurtful. Do we really want to explain to a jealous partner about our pre-married lives? What would that bring apart from potential hurt? Do we really want to tell a child that Santa does not exist and remove the Christmas magic? Isn't this belief part of growing up? So as adults I believe we tend to hide the truth, and choose not to reveal all the facts.

Catharina Lohmann said *"why hurt another person with the truth when a polite lie could boost their ego?"* Nyberg suggested that lying, when done carefully, could even be a compassionate alternative to telling the truth!

Other writers tend to be supportive of this line of thought:

"A truth that's told with bad intent, beats all the lies you can invent"
– William Blake

"Tis not enough your counsel still be true; Blunt truths more mischief than nice falsehoods do"
– Alexander Pope

"The truth is an awful weapon of aggression. It is possible to lie, and even to murder, with the truth"
– Alfred Adler

These neatly capture the dilemma we face – namely determining the difference between hiding the truth to be protective or hiding the truth to be deceitful. Alfred North Whitehead, a British mathematician said: *"There are no whole truths; all truths are half-truths. It is trying to treat them as whole truths that play the devil".* The logical progression of this line of thought is to conclude that truth is also a lie, since we have already considered half-truths can be deceptive and may lead to a false conclusion.

Erich Fromm finds that trying to discuss truth as "absolute truth" is sterile and instead that we ought to place emphasis on getting to grips with "optimal truth". He considers truth results out of our need to survive and we instinctively, especially as children, seek out what we want to be true so as to orient ourselves in "a strange and powerful world". In other words, we filter out that information which does not meet our pre-conceived ideas.

But how does all this new knowledge help us in our quest for honesty? Does it allow us to argue that honesty is only about being truthful? I believe not, because honesty is much more than just what we say. And even if there is truth in what we say, we have discovered it can be risky. It is often difficult to find a balance between telling important truths and protecting the feelings and reputations of everyone involved.

So what does this mean for a leader? I think it demonstrates that we have to use our judgement not only about what we say, but also how we act, behave and decide. I am sure that many of us are no longer "true to ourselves", preferring instead to mould our observable life around the confines of societal or corporate expectations, and in doing that internalise the truths not of ourselves but rather those of others. If you are a leader, is this who you want to be? Or would you rather be free to act as you believe is right and be an honest leader?

If your answer is "yes", read on, for now we have discovered honesty is not simply about being truthful, we must consider other aspects. According to the Oxford English Dictionary: *"Honesty refers to a facet of moral character and denotes positive, virtuous attributes such as integrity, truthfulness, and straightforwardness along with the absence of lying, cheating or theft".*

If we were to accept this interpretation, we introduce the idea of morality and virtues. A virtue is all about moral excellence, when we display a positive trait or a pattern of behaviour that we [society] believe to be morally good or "right". The virtue underlines our individual beliefs, opinions and actions.

With this in mind I argue that being honest is about us being able to ensure that we are "doing the right things" and not just "doing things right". Our own personal definition of moral excellence goes beyond simply telling the truth and we are driven by a robust set of virtues that are inherently good. That we make an effort to search out the right path for our dog and not lead it into some dirty ditch.

Is being moral, honest?

Let's go back to our dog metaphor for a moment. A 2010 article in Scientific American entitled "the ethical dog" made an attempt to understand why dogs seem to have such a keen sense of right and wrong. Every dog owner knows that when their pooch breaks rules, their subsequent floppy eared, sad eyed groveling is so pathetic that you cannot help but quickly forgive it. But few of us probably ever take the time to understand why our dog has such a keen sense of right and wrong.

Dogs follow a strict code of conduct when playing – they teach one another the rules of social engagement and build trusting relationships in packs. These packs enable cooperation and division of labour that resemble early human habits. One of the key aspects of pack gaming is honesty – individuals in the pack who do not play fair are eventually ostracised – leading us to conclude that "fair play" is a simple moral system that is hard wired into a dogs genetic code. OK, I admit it is fairly rudimentary, but in many ways we can draw parallels to human society.

For our purposes I will assume that "doing the right things" is our generic driver for moral behaviour. In other words we make an effort to differentiate our intentions, decisions and actions between "good" and "bad" or "right" and "wrong". The problem starts when we start to try to work out who or what decides what is "right" and what is "wrong".

And that is often left to the moral orientation of society and our culture as a whole. This is because morality develops from shared concepts and beliefs and these concepts are often codified to regulate behaviour and define the principles we should follow within our culture or community.

These codes maybe driven by religion (for example, The Nobel Eightfold path in Buddhism, or the Ten Commandments in Christianity), by politics (duty & obligation in a dictatorial state for example), or maybe driven by other factors such as embedded traditions.

Therefore our actions, which are often based on our beliefs, tend to be termed as being moral or immoral according to societal thinking.

Those of us who choose to be moral are branded as having robust "moral fibre", whereas those who indulge in immoral behaviour may be labelled as socially degenerate!

Some psychologists argue that an individual's sense of morality (our sense of the "*right things*") is not only based on culture but also will develop with the experiences we make over time. Some, such as William Damon who studied moral development throughout human lifespans, argue that our moral commitment [to do the right things] arises from the development of a self-identity that is defined by personal moral purpose. In turn, this self-identity leads to self-driven responsibility to decide whether or not to follow the codified behaviours and principles.

If this were true, a natural question would be to ask what happens in the event that our personal experiences lead to a self-identity that is *not* aligned to societal principles of "right" or "wrong", but *are* aligned to a set of personal religious beliefs? (Some religions, such as Judaism for example, permit lies under certain conditions). Does this mean that society brands us as dishonest whilst our church applauds us for following scripture? How can this be? How can being "moral" also be "dishonest"?

Personally I find religion a rather complex system with many apparently contradictory writings, but nevertheless looking to religion always, perhaps conveniently, seems to find an answer. For example, Hinduism does not specifically ban killing, but rather recognises that it "*may be inevitable and indeed necessary*" under certain circumstances.

Philosopher David Hume, in his book "The natural history of religion" stated that, "*the greatest crimes have been found, in many instances, to be compatible with a superstitious piety and devotion; Hence it is justly regarded as unsafe to draw any inference in favour of a man's morals, from the fervour or strictness of his religious exercises, even though he himself believe them sincere*".

I find the comments of Elizabeth Anderson, a Professor of Philosophy and Women's Studies at the University of Michigan, very thought provoking. She argues in her book "If God is Dead, is Everything permitted?" that religion is "*morally inconsistent*". She asks why we think that people would not *know* the difference [between right or wrong] if God did not reveal it to them. She argues that all societies, whether or not they are based on theism, are embedded upon some understanding of morality (except religious observance) that can be found in the Ten Commandments – for example we inherently understand that it is simply wrong to murder.

Considering that mankind understood these basic moral conditions even before we discovered religion, is not morality and honesty therefore based on our experiences of living together rather than religion?

> "Are actions right because God commands them, or does God command because they are right?"

Plato asked "*Are actions right because God commands them, or does God command because they are right?*" If the former is true, then presumably you could follow an action sanctioned by God but one that is not approved by the moral coding of our society. So in theory it could be possible to be honest and dishonest at the same time.

I have no doubt that some of you are already starting to squirm a little with these words – surely, I can't be suggesting that you can be dishonest in the eyes of society yet honest under the eyes of religion? How can (dare?) I suggest that religion is in some way "not entirely honest" and perhaps even immoral? Let's think about it.

IS RELIGION HONEST?

"Whoa, hang on there" I hear you cry! Religion? You really want to write about religion and honesty? Well, yes I do, as like it or not and regardless of our individual beliefs, every religion that I am aware of has some kind of moral basis within which "honesty" finds its roots. Therefore I do not believe that we can spend time considering the possible origins and meaning of honesty if we ignore religion.

Before I upset anyone however, allow me to comment on the perspective I have taken. I take the view that we are all born into a specific denomination, but whilst some of us consider ourselves as "Christian", we may also struggle to understand the true meaning of the words we read within The Bible. Therefore, sometimes we tend to make our interpretations and ask our questions out of intellectual inquiry. This may of course be different than the views expressed by those who are stronger believers and have no need to ask questions.

Just as an aside, and thinking about the book metaphor, I find it an interesting observation that "God" spelled backwards is dog. And according to author W. E. Farbstein *"The dog is mentioned in the Bible eighteen times – the cat not even once"*. That must mean something. There are other writers such as Linda Basquette who has said, *"So many get reformed through religion. I got reformed through my dogs".* Is religion really important to honesty? Or should we study dogs instead?

Obviously not, but being raised as a Christian, I must confess that I am one of those who sometimes struggles to argue that "honorable intentions" are laid out for us in the various scriptures.

Consider for example the actions and words of God in the Bible, especially the Old Testament. They could be easily misunderstood. He routinely punishes people for their sins. He gives women a painful childbirth for the sins of Eve and condemns man to a life of labour for Adams sins (Genesis 3, 16:18). He kills first born male children, commits genocide and ecocide by flooding the planet (Genesis 6:7), sends a plague to the ancients in Israel and condemns the Samarians, by telling them that their children will be *"dashed to the ground, their pregnant women ripped open"* (Hosea 13:16).

Some more committed religious followers may argue that God may do these things because of who He is – we as mere humans on the other hand may not. And that is probably quite fair. But God tells humans amongst other things to put to death adulterers (Lev 20:10), homosexuals (Lev 20:13), and people who work on the Sabbath (Ex 35:2) – an act that may be considered immoral in modern society.

Of course I have handpicked some passages and taken them out of context just to illustrate my own struggle, and this is clearly a biased thing to do. Allow me to indulge in a further thought: if you were to claim you were abducted by aliens and spent a month living in an UFO, I am certain almost everyone would approach the claims critically and would probably be strapping you into a white coat. But why is it when the scriptures and texts claim that a man can walk on water, was born to a Virgin, was resurrected and flew up into the sky, few raise a hand to question this? And if they do, they may be looked on with pity?

I do believe in God and that our path is laid out for us, but I am sure I am not the only one who might ask these questions. I do acknowledge that The Bible (and we will look at this shortly) also contains many passages about truth, honesty and morality and that this is also the basis of all religion. But in illustrating this point, should we not at least accept that The Bible contains, depending upon perspective, both moral and less moral teachings? At the end of the day you must decide whether or not religion helps you to determine what "doing the right things" may be all about.

Of course I am intentionally raising the temperature, but such questions are giving rise to some surprising actions. In 2007, Sweden took the unusual step of making it illegal for schools to teach religious doctrines as if they were true. Prayer remains legal in schools as it is considered that it has no truth value. But everything that takes place on the curriculum's time must be secular. *"Pupils must be protected from every sort of fundamentalism"* said the minister for schools, Jan Björklund at the time.

This meant for example that the origin of the human race has to be taught only from a scientific perspective. Does this mean that politicians do not believe the revelations taught in the various religious texts are realistic? Is it the beginning of the end of religious "honesty"? Or is it simply a way of trying to ensure an open and balanced education for children who must make their own minds up as they get older? Personally, I will root for the last. What about you?

Of course there are religious people who are honest. Just think of your Llocal priest and others who genuinely believe what their holy books tell them and live by those tenets as best as they can. But the above examples do make it difficult, even for the well-intentioned, to avoid asking some simple questions. We all need answers. Some, perhaps the more extreme amongst us, may argue that atheists are more intelligent simply because they believe that the idea that someone can be resurrected from the dead (for example), is simply preposterous with today's scientific knowledge. So they may even go as far as to argue that religion in itself is not honest.

> *"Some argue that atheists are more intelligent simply because they believe that the idea that someone can be resurrected from the dead is simply preposterous"*

Nevertheless and whatever your beliefs, we do find "honesty" is a common thread that is woven into the foundations of many religious beliefs. As a Christian I will not delve into the depths of all the religious beliefs but will instead try to use my limited understanding of Christianity to illustrate my point.

I presume most of you know the fundamental basis to Christianity is that Jesus is the Son of God and was sacrificed for our [mankind's] sins, and subsequently resurrected to grant eternal life to those who believe and trust in God. Today, around one third of the world's population are declared Christians, making it one (if not the) largest religion.

Extracting some components of The Bible we are told "*The scriptures teach we are to be truthful, sincere and free of deceit*" (Col 3:9; Rom 6:17-18). As part of our development, Philippians 4:8 requests the believer to think on such things as "*whatever is true, whatever is noble, whatever is right, whatever is pure...*". The natural conclusion being that Christians should only dwell on living in an absence of deceit.

Often in the Bible, God commands honesty. It is the object of two of the ten commandments. Exodus 20:15-16 says, "*You shall not steal*". "*You shall not give false testimony against your neighbour*". Ephesians 4:25 says, "*Therefore each of you must put off falsehood and speak truthfully to your neighbour, for we are all members of one body".*

Other passages refer to honesty in other ways. For example, in terms of accepting and applying the truth the Bible puts forth *"But when he, the Spirit of truth comes, he will guide you into all the truth. He will not speak on his own; He will speak only what he hears and he will tell you what is yet to come" (John 16:13).* John further wrote *"There is a judge for the one who rejects me and does not accept my words"* which has been interpreted by various experts that the truth is the word used by God, and that this should not be questioned as being dishonest.

The Bible also deals with our honesty in our relationship with one another. The scriptures are replete with instruction as to how we are to treat our fellow men (Matt 7:12). *"So in everything, do to others what you would have them do to you, for this sums up the Law and the Prophets".* According to the Christian faith, "honesty" requires that we be free of prejudice, selfishness, and pride. Honesty necessitates we accept God's word and apply it to our lives.

Based on these short extracts I am sure that many of you would argue that being faithful is the first step to being an honest leader. All I would ask is that you keep an open mind.

In the interests of putting a balanced perspective into these pages, it would be wrong to argue that religion is honest if we did not return to the views of the non-religions, or atheists. Put simply, atheism is the rejection of the belief about the existence of a deity. Kai Nielsen, in an article in the Encyclopedia Britannica in 2011 argued *"the atheist rejects belief in God because it is false or probably false that there is a God... because the concept of such a God is either meaningless, unintelligible, contradictory, incomprehensible, or incoherent... because the concept of God in question is such that it merely masks an atheistic substance – e.g. 'God' is just another name for love, or ... a symbolic term for moral ideals".*

Atheism as a word originates from ancient Greek, aetheos or "without God". Atheists tend to reason their "anti-deity" arguments with social, historical and philosophical rationalisation. The key for atheists is the lack of hard evidence supporting the existence of a deity, or of evil and even on the various revelations that are alleged to have occurred. But then again this is hardly surprising because finding more than anecdotal evidence after 2000 years is challenging for any historian looking to uncover the truths of the past. How can we ever really know what happened?

Christopher Hitchins was probably one of the more famous (or infamous, depending on your point of view) challengers of religion and a self-confessed atheist. Over his many years as an extremely vocal and public defender of the atheist "faith", he stirred many a hornets' nest, questioning the true validity of religion and deities.

In his book "God is not great: How Religion Poisons Everything" he stated *"What can be asserted without evidence can also be dismissed without evidence."* This would appear to indicate that Hitchins supported our earlier idea that "truth" is only "true" when it can be based on fact or reality (correspondence theory).

Perhaps with more controversy he also stated: *"Owners of dogs will have noticed that, if you provide them with food and water and shelter and affection, they will think you are god. Whereas owners of cats are compelled to realise that, if you provide them with food and water and shelter and affection, they draw the conclusion that they are gods".* Religious believers would presumably argue that God is more than a cat, and their belief in the truth of a deity demonstrates openness and true enlightenment.

In contrast, some atheists argue that human beings are driven by hope – "hope dies last". In this respect we are lying to ourselves because of our need to believe in hope and that there is "something" higher and better than us to help through the tough times. Again Christopher Hitchins: *"Faith is the surrender of the mind, it's the surrender of reason, it's the surrender of the only thing that makes us different from other mammals. It's our need to believe and to surrender our scepticism and our reason, our yearning to discard that and put all our trust or faith in someone or something".*

Others, such as Elizabeth Anderson argue that we would not *care* about doing the right things (being honest) if we were not given a promise of salvation for good behaviour and damnation for bad behaviour. With this view in mind, some suggest that religion is used as the purveyor of all things "honest" using divine sanction to ensure morality. In this instance atheists argue that people do not care what is "right" or "wrong" if God did not make it so. Therefore, are non-believers more likely to be truthful with themselves and also more dishonest because there is no threat of damnation behind them?

Interestingly, people do seem to be stepping back and asking questions. A Gallup poll in 2007, measuring the impact of atheism in the USA, found that approximately 13% did not believe in a deity and were self-confessed atheists. This represented almost a doubling from a similar poll 10 years earlier. Furthermore, when asked how important religion was, whilst 56% of respondents said that religion was "very important" in their own lives, this represented a decline of 14% when compared to the mid-1960's.

Does this mean that while people may believe in God, they are less interested in following the doctrines of religion? Does it mean that people are today more honest about themselves and are happy to admit that there may be something "not quite right" about the religious teachings? Does it mean that religion is no longer seen as the "honest" guide it once was?

Far from it for me to be the judge – I am only here to present a short summary of the potential meaning and understanding of "honesty", and in doing so provoke thought in terms of whether or not "religion" is honest.

Only you can decide if religion is honest, or a guide to "doing the right things", or whether it is all baloney and you would prefer to adhere to the words of Dianne Narciso, author of "Like Rolling Uphill, Realising the Honesty of atheism": *"There's a trigger, somewhere in the human brain, I'm sure, that people just miss. Their thinking dances around it, avoiding logic by every means possible. One day though, for some of us, something hits it. Someone says something like, "I don't know how we got here and neither do you", and the trigger fires, and they suddenly, though too often only briefly, understand lack of knowledge, lack of certainty, lack of belief. They get that it's all just different stories: the Jewish story, the Christian story, the Muslim story, the Hindu story, the Wiccan story; and they get that the atheist just doesn't believe the stories are true".*

So if some authors argue that religion is "not true" what about lies? Can we lie for honest reasons?

HONEST LIES

At this stage it seems we have uncovered a dilemma – one can be honest and dishonest at the same time, depending upon your religious perspective and moral purpose. So we could ask ourselves another question – is lying dishonest?

On the face of it and without me wasting your time, we could presumably answer immediately and agree that lying is certainly dishonest – it's about hiding the truth isn't it, and that is "wrong". Right? Not sure. Think about what I just wrote – that we can follow our beliefs and act accordingly, but those actions, whilst considered moral by religion can be seen as immoral in society. In other words we can be simultaneously honest and dishonest. So presumably then, the converse maybe true – can we lie and still be honest?

Theoretically yes. Dishonesty in literal terms is to *"fake reality"* (Miriam Webster). But dishonesty is not necessarily the same as lying or deceit. To lie is *"to make an untrue statement with the intention to deceive"* (Miriam Webster).

A simple example – you are captured by an enemy in war time and are asked for information concerning certain military targets. You know that one of these targets is fundamental to military success on your side, and you are also aware of a horrible loss of life if it is destroyed. You have the choice – you provide the information or you lie to protect your country. Morally you know it is wrong to be dishonest, but do you tell the truth?

Presumably most of us would lie in this situation; we would provide false information, but justify this with moral reasoning. In this instance this lie could be seen as an "honest lie", because it is only the w*ords* that are dishonest, but the *intention* is honest. Some may this this as being dishonest, rather than a lie. So, can we already conclude that you can have honest lies?

Well, kind of. Let's look again at the above scenario, but from the perspective of the enemy. He receives this information but realises it is a lie – further it is not an honest lie, as from his perspective it was given to him with the intention to deceive. So which is correct? Is a lie honest or dishonest? Well the answer to that seems to be found in whether or not we can distance ourselves from the lie in the first place.

In a paper entitled "Dishonest deed, clear conscious", (Shu, L; Gina, F; Bazzerman, M) the authors refer to a study by Bandura in 1990 & 1999 that argued that people who lie or behave dishonestly, explain their actions as a result of moral disengagement. This is a process of "*persuading oneself that the questionable behaviour is actually morally permissible*". This is not the same as making dishonest behaviour desirable, but rather by "distancing" oneself, it becomes "ok".

"We are not lying if our words are intended to achieve some higher moral purpose"

This level of permissible behaviour is achieved "*... by portraying unethical behaviour as serving a moral purpose, by attributing behaviour to external cues, by distorting the consequences of behaviour, or by dehumanising victims of unethical behaviour. Together, these ways [serve] to morally disengage and explain how individuals recode their actions to appear less immoral*".

In other words, depending on perspective, we may consider that we are not lying if our words are intended to achieve some higher moral purpose and we have disabled our mechanism of self-condemnation and disengaged from the consequences of our actions.

Bandura proposes several steps to becoming morally disengaged:

Moral justification: It was done for a greater good.

Advantageous comparison: Others have done worse things.

Euphemistic label: It sounds better if you call it something else.

Minimising or ignoring the consequences: It wasn't that bad.

Dehumanisation: It was done to one of "them".

Attribution of blame: Iit was what they deserved.

Displacement of responsibility: I did what I was told to do.

Diffusion of responsibility: Everyone else was doing it.

If this is the case, the dishonest liars amongst us can be happy – if you can lie with one of the above arguments in mind then you have successfully disengaged from your actions and you can be free of guilt. Or you can stay with me and accept that this is ridiculous as it is not OK to lie.

But let me also be fair and accept that there is probably a stage when someone crosses the line between a lie with good intentions and a lie with intentional deceit. Here I will use the idea of moral justification to extend this line of thought. If a political or military leader wanted to go to war and kill "the enemy", and they argue that the enemy has chemical weapons or is oppressing the civilians, then their request may well be justifiable, "moral" even.

Think about Syria in 2012. For months the Syrian President Bashar al-Assad has used his armed forces to blatantly murder over 40,000 civilians, including non-combative women and children to protect his government. Is that right? Should we have intervened to bring a swift if brutal end to a murderous regime?

If your answer is yes, and you do not consciously disengage and even actively justify your decision, then you are arguably a dishonest liar because you are not only faking reality (it is OK to kill) but also not making any effort to disengage yourself from what you know to be an immoral action (regardless of who you are killing, it is not permitted from a moral perspective no matter how many reasons you can find). Therefore I would argue that the process of disengagement can help you turn an immoral decision into a moral or honest lie.

The media provides us with many interesting discussion examples of lies and honesty. John Swainton, Chief of Staff of the New York Times back in 1870 stated during his retirement party *"there is not one of you who would dare to write his honest opinion... the business of a journalist now is to destroy the truth, to lie outright, to pervert"*. Which is ironic when one considers that around 135 years later, the Company policy on ethics in Journalism from the very same newspaper amounts to some 139 paragraphs of do's and don'ts and states *"Companywide, our goal is to cover the news impartially and to treat readers, news sources, advertisers and all parts of our society fairly and openly, and to be seen as doing so"*.

So which statement is correct? They both come from sources within the same newspaper, just separated by time. Which would you prefer to believe and which *do* you believe? Not difficult to decide is it?!

The "Society of Professional Journalists" own ethical handbook states "*Journalists should be honest, fair and courageous in gathering, reporting and interpreting information.*" And "*Make certain that headlines, news teases and promotional material, photos, video, audio, graphics, sound bites and quotations do not misrepresent. They should not oversimplify or highlight incidents out of context.*" Now, if we were to read these in isolation we might view the media as a paragon of virtue and trust. But we all know that is not true.

Take for example News Corporation, the global media empire of Rupert Murdoch. A few years ago, the chairman Rupert Murdoch wrote in his forward to the companies' then new code of conduct: "*This public trust is our Company's most valuable asset: one earned every day through our scrupulous adherence to the principles of integrity and fair dealing.*" They use the word "trust" in 4 key segments of their new 56 page book: "*trust in the workplace*", "*trust in the integrity of our employees*", "*trust in our business ethics*" and "*trust in the law*".

However, in the same year that News Corporation released their code of conduct, they were also accused of police bribery and phone hacking of selected celebrities, the Royal Family, various other prominent figures and even victims of bomb attacks in an effort to get exclusive and sensational stories.

The resultant charges initiated a scandal so deep as to shut down one of the oldest British Tabloid newspapers "The News of the World", meaning the loss of 200 jobs, millions in advertising revenues and a flurry of international investigations into the conduct of this and other News Corp. titles. I wonder how much the media can really be trusted?

Rupert Murdoch – An honest leader?

Who is he?

Murdoch is founder, chairman and chief executive of the world's second largest media company, News Corporation. In this position he is by any description one of the most prominent media moguls of the commercial world.

What does he do?

He masterminds the business strategy of the different media divisions of News Corporation, including newspapers, magazines, TV & film and book publishing. Companies and titles under his influence include many household names such as The Times newspaper, ABC television, Sky, Star TV and 20th century fox.

In the annual report the organisation describes itself as *"the only vertically integrated Media Company on a global scale"* and today reports revenues in excess of $30 billion across 175 newspapers, over 20 TV channels, 4 distribution networks and a major book publisher, Harper Collins. The New York Times classed Murdoch as *"The most powerful figure in English language media"*.

What's interesting about him?

Murdoch lives and breathes for the success of the organisation. He is a brilliant pioneer and speculator with an uncanny ability to sniff out the next big thing in media industry.

His character and values have given Murdoch his unique reputation. He has a demanding management style, is willing to take risks and pays fierce attention to financial details. He has a singular approach that focuses around creating business opportunity – his way. Richard Searby, Murdoch's school friend and later a director of the company, said: *"Most boards meet to make decisions. News Corp's board meets to ratify Murdoch's"*.

From the earliest days he has attempted to cash in on and create opportunity. For instance when a competitor offered to buy his newspaper "Adelaide News", Murdoch published the offer letter with the headlines "Bid for press monopoly". Such stirring headlines have marked his approach to business throughout his career.

Murdoch has called himself a catalyst for change and treats business like a battle, which he must win at any cost.

That's why his global newspapers backed the Iraq war. That's why he supported Thatcher, Bush and Reagan. He is an opportunist who likes to back winners. He studies the polls, sniffs the air and backs those who will prevail, especially if it is likely to be good for his business – politicians can open doors to power. For example it is said that he met Gordon Brown 17 times in 12 years – and met Tony Blair for lunch, dinner, teas and chats 31 times in 9 years. And it paid off – his $12 billon takeover of competitor BSkyB, a satellite broadcasting company, was approved despite this giving him virtual monopolistic control of UK satellite TV.

It is said that Murdoch never rests. Neil Chenoweth, an Australian financial journalist, once said *"this is a guy who has to keep moving. In half a century of building News Corp., he has left everyone and everything behind. That applies to ideas. That applies to friends... he'll do whatever he has to do to get the next deal done"*. And that is also a specific recognisable trait of Murdoch.

Is he an honest leader?

Tough question. On one side many consider Murdoch as a true entrepreneur of the media world, having gradually built a global empire with his quick thinking and creativity; writing and exposing headlines and scandals that underlined his belief that the media was a guarantor of democracy. He played a crucial part in cementing Margaret Thatcher's political power and helped break the stranglehold of the Unions at the time. His role in breaking the print unions when he moved his operation to Wapping is still hailed as a brave blow for quality journalism.

But some see him only as a corporate tyrant, bully and a ruthless leader who would expose anyone and anything to get his way. For instance, some may question how topless girls in newspapers such as "The Sun" demonstrate a moralistic thinking and can be any good for society. He arguably launched the age when investigative journalism, supposedly undertaken in the public interest, shed any integrity and became only instructive journalism when nothing, however personal, was a secret anymore.

These actions have drawn criticism that journalism has been replaced by vulgarity, tabloid gossip and sensation seeking stories that have earned Murdoch the name of "Dirty Digger".

Even his private life bears comparison to his tabloids. He has been married 3 times and he himself caused interesting headlines when he married a TV Executive 36 years his junior – and to make this happen ditched his wife of 31 years just 3 weeks prior. I wonder how much moral thinking was involved here.

At over 80, Murdoch must eventually slow down or die. But he still shows no sign of doing either. In the Chairman's letter to the 2012 annual report, Murdoch pushes all to one side. His justification is business success: *"Over the years, I have become accustomed to the noise and negativism of the naysayers. Time and again we have done what they said was impossible: from launching the first national newspaper in Australia to building a fourth broadcast network in America to establishing a great television company in Britain. So my advice is this: Don't judge us the way you would a conventional company. We're a company that thrives on challenges. Our record bears this out"*. And indeed it did as he announced another double digit increase in return to stockholders. This is ultimately all investors care about regardless of the scandals and approach that sit behind the return.

But it is not only the media where we can find traces of dishonesty. In California for example, there is a local by-law that forbids corporations from intentionally deceiving people in their commercial statements, as Nike discovered back in the late 1990's. At that time Nike launched a large PR campaign to convince the public that they had cleaned up their subcontractors practices of using sweatshop labour in Asian markets.

It proceeded to take out full-page ads proclaiming its workers were not unfairly treated and underpaid. However, an alert activist, Marc Kasky argued that Nike were blatantly disregarding the "truth in advertising" law and pressed charges. He and other critics at the time argued that many workers could not afford to buy the items they were making – at the time Honduran factory workers were paid $0.24 for a sweatshirt and $0.15 for a long sleeve t-shirt. That was equal to a purchasing power of $0.50 in the USA.

Despite some early success for Nike and getting the case dismissed, it reappeared in the California supreme court in 2002, when four of the seven judges overturned the dismissal and stated that when a corporation makes *"factual representations about its own products or its operations, it must speak truthfully"*.

Nike went on to lose their case in the California Supreme court and agreed a settlement of $1.5 million that was paid to the Fair Labour Association. In its defence it argued that a corporation should have the same free speech as any individual – they argued that if an individual is allowed to say to another "that looks good on you", then why cannot a corporation have the same privilege in its PR? The counter argument being in the case of Nike we are not talking about people, but rather an organisation arguing for the right to deceive.

Thom Hartmann, in an article entitled "Now corporations claim the right to lie" published at the time of the Nike case, argued that corporations are not breathing, living things that can feel pain, but rather an entity that does not need food to live or water to drink, and that they can change their appearance in a day or rip off a part of themselves and create something entirely new. Therefore they cannot be classed as people and cannot have the same rights. However, the law in some countries disagrees and the "corporate person" is an accepted legal term, providing in effect the right for corporations to lie.

But let's move away from Nike, because lies in advertising are only one aspect. Do companies lie per se? Well, there is some evidence that would appear to show that they do. For example take a few minutes to consider some of the oft-heard statements below.

Things we might hear from "big" companies:

"We have an entrepreneurial spirit here"
"People are our greatest resource"
"We say let the market place decide"

Things we might hear from small and mid-size companies:

"We choose to stay small"
"The boss is one of the guys"

Things we might hear from marketing companies:

"We treat all customers as if they were the most important"

Things we might hear from software companies:

"The programme is fully tested and bug free"
"We're working on the documentation"
"Of course it can be easily modified"

Do any of these ring a bell? Of course! We have all experienced, or maybe ourselves invented these statements at one time or another. Let's be realistic – behind every corporation is a person. People lie, with or without intent. We already know that lying is often justified on moral grounds, or simply to save face. It's a fact of life. Therefore, if people lie, one can also assume that the PR streaming out of a corporation will sometimes be less truthful than it should.

An amusing, perhaps slightly cynical but nevertheless thought provoking read is a book by "Warlizard" called "8 corporate lies you think are true but aren't". From some perspectives (bitter employees!) the pages certainly give food for thought. How many times for example have you heard statements such as:

"You are being groomed for promotion"
"We support your work life balance"
"You need certification / training / degrees to get promoted"
"We like to promote from within"
"Human resources is here to help you"

Sound horribly familiar? The thing about corporate lies, according to the book, is that they are almost universally believed, from the small people turning the wheels all the way up the food chain to the top. And it is not until you get to the top that you realise you were being led down a garden path with ridiculous statements such as those above. They are gestated in Human Resources to make us feel good – signed up to by senior leaders, repeated by managers and believed by employees.

But they are not really true – rather the lies exist to make you work harder. If people believe that with hard work, application of skills, studying and perhaps a wee bit of luck that they will advance, then why tell them the truth?

Think about it – do you come in early, go home late, and work like hell for 10 years just to stay in the same position? No! You believe that with hard work you will be rewarded. Sure, occasionally it can happen – but let's be realistic – any advance in your career is probably at the expense of someone else. Welcome, says the book, to corporate reality, where a company exists only for one purpose – making money.

Warlizard asks if you really think that the stockholders and owners of a company care how happy you are? Really? The only reason it matters is because happy employees work harder and are more productive. If you are not productive enough, you are told to leave, or you are put on the radar as a potential "c" case. Which between the lines means, *"improve or leave"*. Trying to get employees happy is more important than the horrible alternative – replacing the employee because that is more expensive than finding and training a new hire.

So let's put this in a nutshell – it is easier for a corporation to convince you that you're going somewhere. That you're valued and you're needed. Each lie will get you to work harder – the lies contain maybe a small element of truth, or a small handful of people can be found to exemplify the hope behind the lie, meaning that the "great majority" will believe it as being their "truth" too – *"if good stuff can happen to them then it can happen to me"* – right? Wrong. If a company needs to lay off 2,000 people it will do so. If it wants to cut bonuses, it will. If it wants to fire people, it will.

> *"Do you really think that the stockholders and owners of a company care how happy you are?"*

But the lying appears not to just come from management. Sure the rot starts at the top, but in a survey carried out by pollsters YouGov for software giant Microsoft in 2005, it was found that three quarters of workers feel they are forced to lie at work, with over half owning up to what Microsoft termed as "blagging" (deceitful informal conversation).

According to the survey, almost two-thirds of people blamed a lack of information for their "blagging", while half felt under unreasonable time pressures and almost a quarter were not sure that the information they were expected to act upon was correct.

"If workers are regularly forced to act on incomplete information and in unreasonable timeframes, as their answers reveal, then how can management know they are acting correctly?" Microsoft asked. But

who's to blame? The management team for gestating a lying culture, or the employee for perpetuating it?

Now that I have effectively accused all organisations and their employees of lying to protect their own interests, let us also consider another perspective – many organisations these days are driven by robust and admirable codes of conduct and corporate governance. Most blue chips discuss social responsibility in their annual reports and do make a visible effort to make the workplace a great place to be, for example through various employee engagement initiatives.

After all, much as we could argue that happy employees are productive employees, we could also argue that a great workplace attracts great people who can deliver great service – and yes whilst this drives productivity, what's wrong with being happy at work – after all, the majority of us must work for at least 10 hours a day, 5 days a week, 50 weeks a year for 40 years – and that's just the official bit! – so why the hell should it not be enjoyable and why should we not hope for improvements in our careers? Hope dies last, right?

So perhaps it would be more balanced to wonder if there are other factors that drive corporate lies. One reason can certainly be found in the roots of today's investment culture. Today investors reward good short-term financial performance with stock purchases and high corporate valuations. Meaning stockowners get richer and investors happier. And let's be realistic – wall street sized bonuses do not get paid for telling the truth, but rather for generating profit. This ethos, when coupled with a corporate culture that is margin driven, may produce a climate within which balance sheet restatements may be discovered. But this should not be an excuse to bend the truth.

> *"Wall street sized bonuses do not get paid for telling the truth, but rather for generating profit"*

The Huron consulting group in a study in 2003 found that the number of organisations in the US that re-stated their financial records had risen to 323 in 2003, up from 270 in 2000. In part this was down to people and system mistakes, but new requirements on corporate vigilance may also have been driving this trend. Some however were re-stated due to "earnings management" (fraud) techniques.

Indeed, we continue to read about major organisations that deliberately mislead investors – the Italian giant Parmalat for instance had not only €14 billion in debt, but also had an imaginary €3.9 billion bank account in the Bank of America, allowing it to effectively falsify its true financial state. Despite verification by auditors, the reports of other large corporations such as Cendant, Tyco International and Enron all contained irregularities.

Cendant for instance allegedly booked $500 million in fake revenue over 3 years. Tyco was investigated for hiding debt and thus inflating revenue reports. And we all know what happened at Enron. Each company systematically and carefully hid lies amongst truths, inflated good numbers and hid the bad.

So what does this mean? Can any corporation be trusted? It appears that from the perspective of an employee or that of an investor, the "truth" may be hard to find. But what about the perspective of the customer? Do corporations lie to them as well? Of course they do!

Theodore Levitt, author of "Marketing Myopia", an article published in the Harvard Business review, claimed corporations focus too much on product and not enough on customers. He wrote "*selling concerns itself with the tricks and techniques of getting people to exchange their cash for your product*".

"*Sales*", he said, "*does not... view the entire business process as consisting of a tightly integrated effort to discover, create, arouse, and satisfy customer needs. The customer is somebody 'out there' who, with proper cunning, can be separated from his or her loose change.*" So one would assume that if sales people think along these lines, then maybe it's not too much of a stretch to assume that a corporate sales strategy would also include a little white lie or two.

Don't be shocked! You knew this really, right? Consider some examples. Back in 2008 a US TV organisation, Cablevision wrote to all its TV subscribers claiming the Federal Communications Commission (FCC) will require all subscribers to upgrade to digital cable boxes within the year. At the time the monthly price for a digital cable box was $6.50, plus an extra $10.95 for digital service. So upgrading was going to cost $17.45 per customer – of which they had 40 million!

Fact is, the claim about the FCC was a complete fabrication, but

Cablevision had decided to migrate several of their channels to the digital service and wanted their customers to follow suit. Do the math! Are customers really so addicted to TV that they are happy to just pay the price? Some did.

Allegedly Apple employees once told customers that unlocking their iPhone can fry the antenna. And at Office Depot times were real tough back in 2009 when it was discovered by Laptop Online that employees knowingly told their customers that they were out of stock of laptops if they did not purchase extended protection plans or other options such as cables and modems. Quoting one employee *"Once I was talking to the customer and, while I am actually speaking, my manager comes on the radio and tells me to say it is out of stock if they aren't getting anything with it"*.

But surely this can't be right? It cannot be that a sales person just wants to clock up sales commissions and does not care about customer satisfaction. Sales should be based on ethics, and in this respect what organisations or sales people do is certainly important. But I also recommend that you listen carefully to what they *do not* do or say.

Google (as I did when researching for this book) *"companies that lie"* and you'll get pages and pages of opinions about companies that lie. Are these bloggers/writers telling the truth? Who is really doing the lying? I have no clue. A sensible starting point would presumably be to assume that everyone is lying somehow about something. Even if they know it, admit it, justify it or not.

I am sure that by now you will have drawn your own conclusions about our question – "are lies honest". But I am struggling to think of anything other than an emphatic "no". How can they be, even if done for moral reasons? Surely it cannot be that we have to disengage our moral thinking to justify a lie. Somehow, this goes against the grain of common sense. An honest leader does not lie. Period.

Mutual trust and shared interest – games on the international stage

When the last President of China, Hu Jintao met with US President Obama in early 2012 they spoke of the need to continue with long-term cooperation and mutual trust. But Obama, back in 2008 and as a Presidential candidate said *"America and China have developed a mature wide ranging relationship of 30 plus years. Yet we still have some serious work to do if we are to create the level of mutual trust necessary for long term cooperation in a rapidly changing region".*

Why would he say that? What exactly is mutual trust, and is it even possible between these, or for that matter, any two nations? Mutual trust is a feeling experienced by both parties and is a two way street – you trust us, we trust you. It comes from experience and exists when one party does not surprise the other. It is a kind of basis that states that both sides believe the other, and see each other as credible partners. It is not blind faith; but if you can work with someone you trust it saves a lot of heartache, time and energy. But does the US really trust China and vice versa? Probably not.

There are countless examples of attempts at getting mutual trust between these two nations, but none appear to succeed. Ever since the Communists claimed power shortly after the Second World War there has not been too much trust between China and the US. Rather a working cooperation has existed for many years, that has culminated in occasional shared military exercises, such as those demonstrated by the joint movements off the coast of Somalia to combat piracy.

During President Clintons visit in 1998 the two governments defined their relationship as a "strategic partnership". And just to underline this strategic thinking, both governments issued statements that followed the visit of President Jintao to Washington in 2011; *"The United States... welcomes a strong, prosperous, and successful China that plays a greater role in world affairs. China welcomes the United States as an Asia-Pacific nation that contributes to peace, stability and prosperity in the region."* Clearly, nothing has really changed in the intervening years.

This is not mutual trust – the threat of nuclear war as a result of escalated tensions keeps this at bay, and at best the term "neither friend nor enemy" seems most fitting. Perhaps the closest to mutual trust two nations can get is illustrated between Britain and America.

The relationship between the two remains strong. When the US asks the UK to jump, it invariably does. In 1984 Margaret Thatcher said in her first meeting with Mikhail Gorbachev "*I am an ally of the United States. We believe in the same things, we believe passionately in the battle of ideas, we will defend them to the hilt. Never try to separate me from them*".

But America's relationship with all other nations is at best shared interest. This is less about trust and more about sharing a common ground and objectives. For example it is in the interest of Saudi Arabia to sell oil to the US. The more it sells the more income it gets. As one of the world's largest oil consumers it is in the interest of the US to receive oil to support economic growth. And so Saudi Arabia is a perfect example of shared interest for the US. Even though the Saudi state practices absolute monarchy versus democracy and functions somewhat differently, the two became "friends" – with a commonly shared interest focused around black gold.

Mutual trust is difficult to achieve. It mostly comes as a result of a great relationship that starts out with shared interest. Washington and Beijing should simply realise that and build on a realistic premise of shared interest to start.

DO WE MANIPULATE HONESTY?

Where are we on our journey? Well, we appear to have no black and white decision about what "honesty" actually is. After all, we have realised that it is perhaps OK to lie under the right circumstances and that not all individuals share the same truth. It appears that some organisations are not necessarily the paragons of virtue we may have hoped and some psychologists seem to disagree amongst themselves about what truth is. Even the reliable bastion of religion appears to be littered with some rather contradictory statements about how we may view "right" or "wrong".

We know a dog cannot lie. And we know this is not true of people who are able to manipulate the truth. Therefore, perhaps it is better for us not to ask "what is honesty", but rather try to understand if it is possible for us to "adjust" how honest we are.

Is it possible for example to have different kinds of lies that are "more or less truthful", and can be used depending on the scenario we face? Is it possible to consciously control how much we lie, or is it a sub-conscious habitual action? Does your chosen level of honesty depend on personal intelligence, upbringing or attitude? Or is it more simply related to situation and experience?

The question now is how much truth is told to avoid serious trouble? Let's try this out. How honest are you? Most people think they are pretty honest, but are we? Take the quiz below and record your answers.

1. Your best friend of 10 years asks you if she looks good in her new dress. You also know she has a very nervous disposition and is very sensitive to criticism. In fact the last time she was lied to, she became so upset she had quite a serious accident and you are very worried about her level headed ability to handle negative news. You:

a. Tell her she looks good, even though the dress leaves her looking all pale and washed out.
b. Advise her to get a tan. That will help with the colouring. However, don't tell her why. It will just hurt her feelings.
c. Tell her to return the awful dress. She can look better, and you'll help her shop for the right one.

2. You are a big sports fan and enjoy and believe in fair competition. However, a training friend of many years tells you he's been using steroids, and he wants you to promise not to tell anyone. He has been training hard for a forthcoming sports event and stands a good chance of winning. If he does win it will also bring a once in a lifetime career breakthrough for him. You:

a. Promise, then tell another colleague.

b. Promise and don't tell anyone.

c. Don't promise. You know he's in trouble and he really needs help.

3. You get out of the store you visit nearly every day and realise the cashier gave you an extra €5 in change. You:

a. Go home. Hooray! An extra €5. It's the cashier's fault, after all.

b. Slip the €5 back on the counter by the cashier.

c. Give the money back to the cashier so she can put it back into the till.

4. When the boss tells you he is going to increase your salary more than the others in the same team for the same job, do you:

a. Shut up, take the promotion and just say thanks, justifying this as an extra bonus for your own loyalty and hard work

b. Offer him/her some extra time or hours in return

c. Refuse the pay rise as it is unfair against the others

5. You overhear some people talking and whispering about a friend of yours. You don't say anything, but later your friend asks you if people were taking about her. You:

a. Tell her you haven't heard anything. Why hurt her feelings?

b. Tell her you heard something, but sugar-coat it.

c. Tell her what you heard and help her solve the problem.

Scoring Key

Give yourself the following points for each answer:

A=1

B=2

C=3

5 – 7: You are a moral liar, meaning you often lie to protect the feelings of others or protect your standing among friends. While you don't lie for the sake of lying, you can find ways of telling the truth or at least justifying an "honestly intended" lie.

10 – 12: You usually only lie when it depends on someone's feelings. You see this as a lie out of necessity. A white lie perhaps, but you do feel occasionally guilty depending on the circumstances.

12 – 15: You are a truth-monger and prefer to be direct. You tend to be morally driven and do not appreciate being lied too.

This dilemma – how *much* truth do we tell, or how honest do we want to be – we carry forward into adult hood. As we get older we are faced with hundreds of situations every day. Do we lie or not? If yes, "how much" do we lie? Consider the different kinds of lies below, and ask yourself if you recognise or use them:

Barefaced lie: A barefaced (or bald-faced) lie is, put simply, when we lie with a straight face. Our body language, tonality and all aspects except the words correspond to us telling the truth.

Bluffing: We all bluff and we do it regularly – when we do so we infer that we have a capability or something else that we do not actually possess. We do it in poker. We do it on our CV or in a job interview. We may even do it amongst friends in a bar when trying to create an image for ourselves. Ultimately however, bluffing is an act of deception – but one that is rarely seen as immoral.

Contextual lie: This is when we take part of the truth and state it out of context, knowing that without complete information, we can give a false impression. Hence, this may give a feeling that we are "holding something back" in our conversation.

Exaggeration: This occurs when we "stretch the truth" and make something appear more powerful, meaningful, or real than it actually is.

Fib: This is when we tell a lie with no malicious intent and little consequence. Saying that, unlike a white lie, fibs do not always mean well.

Lying: Most unpleasant this one – put simply we are lying face-to-face, possibly combined with a smile!

Puffery: Often found in advertising and publicity announcements, such as "the highest quality at the lowest price" or "always votes in the best interest of all the people". Such statements are unlikely to be true – but cannot be proven false and therefore do not violate trade laws, especially as the consumer is expected to also realise that it is not the absolute truth.

White lies: These are minor lies, which we may even use to protect others in the long term. A common version of a white lie is to tell only part of the truth, therefore not be suspected of lying, yet also conceal something else, to avoid awkward questions. For example, "You look wonderful in that dress darling". Perhaps she did. But not anymore!

These many kinds of lie indicate that it is actually more common to find levels of dishonesty – or put another way "different kinds of lies" – than it is to find examples of absolute honesty or dishonesty. Even Aristotle believed no general rule on lying was possible, because anyone who did lie would never be believed again.

Modern writers such as Iain King in his book "How to make good decisions and be right all the time" argue that most people are in a real conundrum when it comes to figuring out the difference between "right and wrong", and tend to leave the answers to the powers that be – regardless of whether they are judges, politicians or in religion. He argues that in this process some people even have different rules for different people "*it's OK for them to do that but not me*". This implies that levels of dishonesty are not only normal, but that it's also OK because we ourselves do not know how far we should go.

King goes further and devotes a whole chapter to explaining when it is OK to lie and actually suggests lying is possible when the pay-off from lying is greater than the risk of being caught: *"Deceive only if you can change behaviour in a way worth more than the trust you would lose"*. King also believes a lie is justifiable when the truth will create inappropriate reactions from others and lying becomes necessary and acceptable.

But is this *really* the only answer? I am not sure, but in writing this book I had many discussions about the tendency of humans to lie, when, how and why. I am sure you have these discussions too. At the end of the day, I presume (hope?) that most of us do not go through life figuring out how to manipulate and lie only for personal gain. We all have our own personal radar about what is right or wrong, good or bad and on the whole try to live honest lives, whatever that may mean. Perhaps, a more apt question is whether or not we lie to ourselves? Does this process of self-justification *"oh it's OK this time, no-one will know"* make it alright to lie? Do we lie so much and give it so little thought that we do not even know we are lying anymore?

A study recently published in Psychological Science found that we are more likely to tell a lie when we do not have time to work out if it is right or wrong to do so. Past work has shown that many of us have a greater tendency to lie when it is in our own interest, making it easier to justify lying to ourselves. Research for this study showed that with financial gain and little time to make a decision, many of us will have an increased tendency to lie.

The study analysed the frequency of participants to tell a lie when throwing a dice and reporting the number thrown within a given time frame. The number the participants reported could however be real or false. The participants could earn money depending on the value of the dice on subsequent throws and whether any lie from the first roll was discovered or not. The research found that the tendency to lie rose the greater the earning potential and the less the time to report on their dice roll.

Whilst this is of course a lab experiment it does show interesting tendencies – Professor Shalvi, a co-author of the research said *"according to our theory, people act first upon self-serving instincts and only with time do they consider what socially acceptable behaviour is*". The message for leaders from this is to keep an open mind, give plenty of time and not to push followers into a corner if we are wishing to increase the likelihood of not getting false statements. *"People usually know it is wrong to lie – they just need time to do the right thing"* said Shalvi. This could be an especially important message to mediators for example.

But why is all this even necessary? Why do we even feel the need to tell different kinds of lies? Here are some possible reasons.

Avoid harm & conflict: If we tell the truth we may have uncomfortable consequences. Are we ready for these?

Avoid punishment: How many children have an uncanny way of avoiding the truth for fear of retribution from their parents or teachers?

Avoid rejection: How often do we hide the truth to appear more popular to others? This is simply grounded in our own personal insecurities. In some cultures this may be related to a loss of self-esteem or pride, where personal opinions are often masked and the "group thinking" will take over to avoid sticking out. It may be that we even lie to ourselves to avoid a loss of moral – after all, hope is said to die last.

To protect our friends and loved ones: How often do we use flattery just to make them feel better? Or provide an element of hope that things are not as bad as they seem? Or avoid telling the whole truth because we are afraid of hurting someone's feelings?

The fact is we all practice the art of being honest, whether consciously or sub-consciously. The key characteristic about honesty is that it cannot be learned – you are either honest, or you are dishonest. You have a choice about what you say and do. It is always possible to rationalise and justify your own intentions. We know what we do and why. We know the corners we cut and the decisions we make for ourselves. No amount of training or executive coaching will instruct you on how to be honest – but experience will guide you on how to *practice* honesty. And practice starts with intention.

HONEST INTENTIONS

The practice of being honest is a challenging one. On the one hand we can be completely honest, yet on the other we can be the opposite – namely completely dishonest. Respect for others, business and social etiquette often temper the amount of honesty we practice in our everyday communication.

One approach to think about how we practice honesty has been developed by Jon Mertz in the "Leadership Honesty Spectrum" as part of his studies on character based leadership.

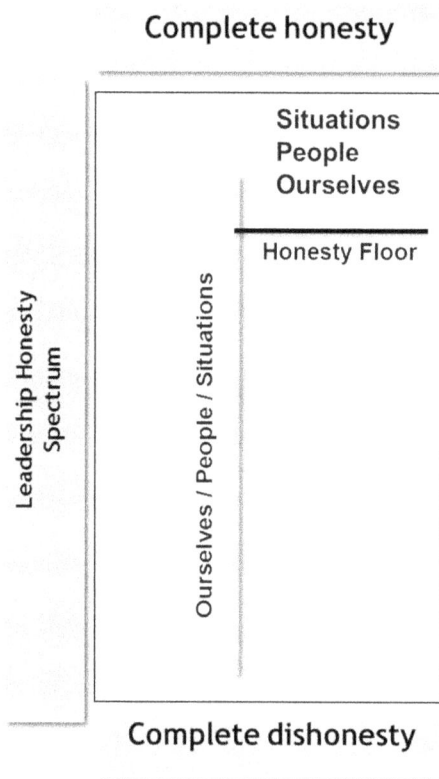

"Leadership Honesty spectrum" by Jon Mertz 2012

In this approach Mertz argues that each individual is aware of the concept of being completely honest and completely dishonest. Somewhere within this boundary we create for ourselves an "acceptable level" of honesty that we decide to practice, which Mertz terms the "honesty floor". The positioning of this floor may vary according to the situation we are facing, the people we are dealing with and our own attitude and personality at the time.

Situations: Under normal circumstances most of us can assess, digest and resolve the daily situations that we are presented with. We become experienced over time at dealing with these events and decide how they can be handled and the amount of honesty we need to practice to resolve them.

However, we are perhaps rarely completely honest because of our fear of facing reality. We struggle to face the ugly truth that something unpleasant may have to be done or said to find a resolution – whether it is admitting we were wrong or dealing with a poor performer for example.

In some cultures the cold hard truth can damage relationships and self-esteem beyond repair. Therefore we shy away from complete honesty and beat around the bush using indirect and friendly conversation and hope the situation just goes away. However, we learn that situations just don't disappear. We need to face them, and if we want to move through them, resolve them.

People: We all have to face difficult people from time to time. Whether it's our neighbour who refuses to clean his dog poop from our driveway, or our boss who criticises our work or the partner who needs you home every day at 1700, our tendency is to be less honest, because we don't want to be uncomfortable or find ourselves in an argument. As Will Rogers, social commentator said *"If you get to thinking you're a person of some influence, try ordering somebody else's dog around"*.

Let's be realistic – having a challenging conversation with someone about a change required, especially if it is about their behaviour, is not easy. Dogs do not like to change, they are who they are. People are no different. We would rather ignore the problems and hope they just fix themselves. This of course does not happen.

An honest way is to demonstrate respect and empathy and to provide examples of how the other person's activity is creating challenges. Through open honest dialogue it should be possible to offer solutions that both can commit to. One solution is AID, a useful guide to a challenging conversation:

A = Action – what is it that someone is doing and/or you have observed

I = Impact – what is the result to you or other stakeholders, how do you feel about the action of the other

D = Desired result – what could we (both) do to find a solution to this challenge

Ourselves: This is where honesty is taken to the extreme. By nature we are not very good at being self-critical and we tend to give ourselves high self-evaluations that would not necessarily be supported by our peers. We are all great at self-affirmation and believing we are doing the right thing.

In the business world this thinking is especially prevalent. In a typical profit and achievement-orientated company where strategies tend to be driven through delivering positive shareholder return, the environment is extremely competitive. Information becomes power. Each leader and employee must be seen to be contributing to the big picture and delivering positive return to the organisation. This tends to generate a "me versus them" culture, as we fight and jostle with our colleagues to achieve our objectives and secure the next promotion (or keep a job). It becomes a world of everyman for themselves and whether knowingly or not, we spend time ensuring that the monkey sits on someone else's desk. *"It must be someone else's mistake, right"?*

Therefore, more often than not we become task orientated. We ask *"how can I deliver on my promises"*, rather than *"how can I deliver better"* or even *"what and why am I delivering and what is the added value of this"*? The danger is that despite our good intentions, our actions often become transactional rather than transformational focused. We start to consciously consider the level of honesty we will use in our conversations, perhaps dialing back on open dialogue if we believe it will not help to achieve our targets.

As Andy Andrews in his book "The Noticer" states, we often judge others by their actions, but ourselves by our intentions. But intention without action is a waste of time. There is no point in intending to be honest if this intention is not followed through! There is no difference between the person who intends to do something and the person who never thinks about it in the first place! Dogs figured this out long ago – say something to a dog without consequent actions in your body language and tonality, and your dog will happily continue with whatever it was doing in the first place.

Of course, no-one usually intends to go to work to fill their day with carefully constructed lies and do a bad job. But let's be honest, if not telling the entire truth helps you shine in that job, perhaps your final actions do not always follow your moral intentions.

Therefore, even though we strive to keep a consistent honesty floor, I believe we are actually in a constant state of flux. Our intentions may be one thing, but in reality our actions are often different and are the result of a conscious choice we make to be honest or dishonest – in every situation and interaction we face. It is however vital to grasp that our personal reputation ultimately rests upon our observable actions and any consequences that arise from those actions; reputation cannot be based on our hidden intentions or choices.

I believe that this model from Mertz can therefore be adapted. We already know that our intentions are influenced by the situation, by the people involved and by our own values and expectations. However, we are always weighing up the potential damage that may be created if we are too honest or dishonest. We perhaps ask ourselves, for example, how much power we may gain or lose from being more or less honest? Or how will my actions propel me forwards or drag me backwards? Or will it be easier or harder to achieve my objectives?

In other words I believe "political sensitivity" should be singled out as an additional filter that must be explicitly considered when making a choice on how honest we wish to be. Therefore my model – let's term it the "Honesty Filter Model" – considers that our actions are determined by our "politically filtered" intentions and choices:

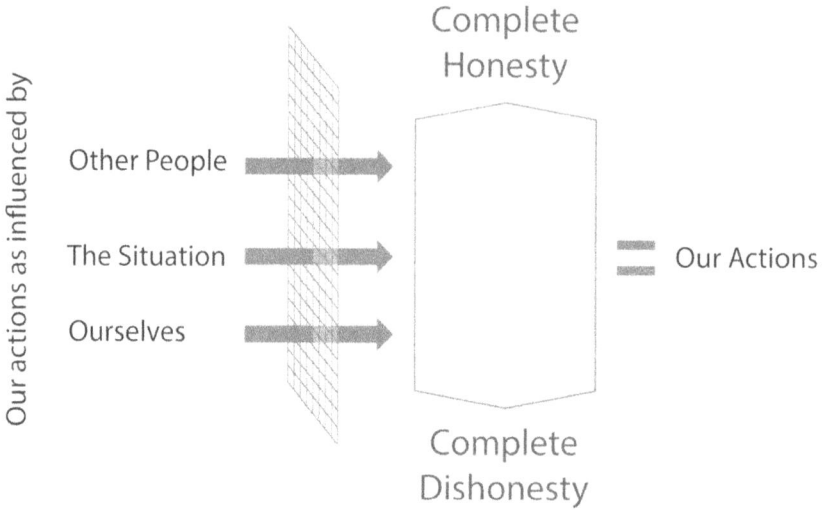

Honesty Filter Model, by David Watkins 2013

Taking all these thoughts into consideration, I wonder if it is possible to predict the level of honesty that someone may or may not demonstrate in a certain situation? This is not the same as watching someone sweat, look down and shuffle their feet when they are telling porkies, because they are *already* lying. More to the point can we predict that someone will be dishonest *before* they lie to us? Can we identify honest from dishonest people? Is there anything out there that we could use as an "indicator" of honesty?

AN HONEST ATTITUDE

Some of us may feel that our attitude may be one such indicator of our dispensation towards honesty. For example, we could argue that those with a bad attitude are more likely to lie than those with a positive attitude. After all, as Lewis Grizzard, US writer and humourist stated *"you call to a dog and a dog will break its neck to get to you. Dogs just want to please. Call to a cat and its attitude is, 'what's in it for me'?"*

An attitude is a tendency to respond in a positive or negative manner to a given set of inputs or ideas. An attitude indicates our level of acceptance for these inputs and influences, our choices of action and response. Our emotions or feelings, combined with our opinion and beliefs are key components that make up our personal attitude.

Attitudes, just like emotions, can therefore be positive and negative, and in each case are displayed with passive or active behaviours. Consider the below table. If we go through our day with a positive attitude we tend to be more open to new ideas and more supportive in our behaviour. Our verbal commentary is likely to be more open and by implication more honest. We demonstrate enthusiasm and will automatically want to share thoughts and ideas. We may wish to encourage honest open dialogue and add value to common efforts.

Conversely, if we are somewhat negative in our attitude we find the opposite. We tend to close up and hide information, keeping our cards close to our chest. We take the view that being too honest may disadvantage our positioning as we seek to undermine or disrupt the efforts of others.

Behaviour	Emotions	How we feel	What we say
Active	Positive	Conviction	"Done it already!"
		Enthusiasm	"100% behind you"
Passive		Interest	"Sounds good, what about..."
Neutral			"ok, but let me think a little"
Passive	Negative	Concern	"Not sure, is there another way?"
		Hostility	"It´s wrong and poorly planned"
Active		Indifference & Avoidance	"what´s the point?"

Inspired by "attitudes in sales" by Overlap Consultores 2011

Therefore, when we come across individuals with a rather "bad attitude", the chances are that they have a tendency to lie that is higher than those with a good open attitude.

Just like attitudes, emotions also play a part in honesty. Daniel Goleman, in his book "Primal Leadership" writes that the emotion of a leader – their "emotional style" – could impact the performance of followers. He linked this into intelligence. He states that higher levels of intelligence and more positive emotions lead to the creation of a trustworthy climate and therefore the task of a leader is *"to make sure that not only he is regularly in an optimistic, authentic and high energy mood, but also that through his chosen actions, his followers feel and act that way too"*. This leads in short to [financial] success. So, with this in mind, we should certainly ask ourselves if intelligence has anything to do with honesty.

INTELLIGENT HONESTY

Some argue that lying may be a sign of individual strength, because to maintain a lie requires intellectual capacity. If this were true does this mean we have to be on the lookout for clever leaders? Are they better liars? Or are they too clever to need to lie?

One way to look at this is to consider the concept of Emotional Intelligence put forward in the 1990's by Daniel Goleman. He argued that higher levels of intelligence created a climate that encourages information sharing, trust and healthy risk taking. The theory finds its roots in the business world and entertains the idea that leaders have not only great technical skills and [probably] a higher IQ, but also higher tendency to display certain characteristics that make them more effective as leaders, such as driving and supporting change, the ability to interact and work with others and the demonstration of initiative and strategic thinking. He linked these characteristics to Emotional Intelligence.

These additional characteristics tend to be more important than pure technical intellect – especially at higher levels of an organisation where less transactional thinking (getting the job done) and more transformational thinking (finding ways of doing the job better) is important. When Goleman studied the differences in the profiles between the star and average performers, he found that 90% of the difference was attributable to these Emotional Intelligence factors.

Looking at Goleman's summary below, I am gratified to realise that some of the items we have considered in our search for honesty such as morals, integrity, attitudes, and trustworthiness can also be found within the components of Emotional Intelligence. I wonder however if those leaders with high EI levels more adept at lying and ready to do it? I will hold onto that thought for now.

Component	Definition	Characteristic
Self-Awareness	The ability to recognise and understand your moods, as well as their impact on others	• Self confidence • Realistic self-assessment • Knowledge of strength and weaknesses
Self-management	The ability to direct this self-awareness for good (or disruption) To think before acting	• Trustworthiness and integrity • Comfort with ambiguity • Openness
Motivation	To work for reasons other than money or status	• Drive • Optimism • Commitment
Empathy	The ability to understand emotions of others To be able to treat others according to their reactions	• Cross cultural sensitivity • Service to clients and customers • Get into the minds of others
Social skills	The ability to build networks and manage relationships	• Effective at leading change • Persuasive

Inspired by Goleman: from "What makes a Leader" HBR 2004

Let's take a look at some of the above components and see if we can identify if a person with high Emotional Intelligence is more likely to be honest (or not).

Self-awareness: Goleman argues that when we are highly self-aware, we recognise not only how our feelings affect ourselves, but how they can affect others and their job performance. There is no reason why this is only important in the business world, because self-awareness extends to our understanding of our personal values and goals. The more self-aware we are the greater the chance we know where we are headed and why. We tend to share our opinions and often tell tales with a smile. We know about our successes and failures, and can articulate our strengths and weaknesses, and especially have a good understanding of what needs to be done.

Goleman's research showed that we do appreciate the candour and trustworthiness that exists around a self-aware individual. If we are self-aware we have a good capability to make a candid assessment of the situation – and talk about it.

> *"We appreciate the candour and trustworthiness that tends to exist around a self-aware individual"*

Oddly however, those of us with high self-awareness may not always be seen as "tough enough" in the business world or to lead others. Take for example the executive who must negotiate with suppliers – they work with scrupulous honesty in all their dealings and therefore cannot always achieve the hard bargain that is expected of them. It may be that occasionally this executive felt he could achieve a better deal by "hiding the truth" about organisational costs, but in the mind of this executive, a partly dishonest approach would mean that his assessment is not candid and in the long run perhaps even damaging once the truth came out and the deal needs re-negotiating.

Self-management: Goleman also argued that those of us with higher Emotional Intelligence display a higher ability to control our emotional impulses. We are able to pick our words more carefully and think before we talk. Those with high levels of self-management do not rush into hasty judgment. From the perspective of "being honest" this is important – those who are less likely to fly off the handle and can

66

control their emotions are more able to create an environment of fairness, respect and trust. If we can demonstrate good self-management we tend also to be more reasonable and less judgmental.

Goleman believes that good self-management enhances integrity, which is not only an organisational strength but also a personal virtue. Many "bad things" can happen to companies or individuals which are the result of impulsive behaviours – people who are impulsive are more likely to succumb to dishonesty, to pad expense accounts, to dip into the till or to exaggerate the profits in their stock market reports. It would appear that intelligent people are better at being honest in this respect.

Motivation: A friend once told me that motivation is broadly made up of 4 "p's". They are Position, Power (earned from that position be it hierarchy, job title, information etc.), Possession (things you have, possibly also as a result of your position) and Personality. The latter is who you are, the sum of your experiences to date, the journey you have taken. Strongly intelligent leaders will be very much aware of this; they know where they want to go, where they are today and what they need to do to get to where they want to be.

Personality is vital. It makes up our motivation to embark on the journey to being honest and start the process to becoming top dog. Whilst the first 3 p's can be removed, no-one can ever change who you are, and emotionally intelligent people are driven by their personal honesty to accept and be truthful to themselves.

Empathy: We have all been struck at one time or another by the apparent absence of understanding displayed by our boss, our friends or even our partners, but empathy in this sense does not mean "are you OK, I am too" nor does it mean that an emotionally intelligent person is trying to adopt someone else's emotions as their own. Rather, I refer to empathy as thoughtfully considering the feelings of another in your everyday actions. It means being open, honest and fair in your dealings with others.

Social skills: In the context of Emotional Intelligence, social skills are intended to infer "friendliness with reason" – the ability of someone to move people in the direction we desire. People with high social skills tend to be adept at managing teams and are especially good persuaders, as a result of their high levels of empathy, self-awareness and self-management.

If we take a few minutes to consider some of these thoughts, it infers that those with high Emotional Intelligence are great people to know. They can in effect use their skills set and empathise with our problems, help us see our goals, say the right things to us at the right time, can control their emotions and probably know what makes you tick. Surely, we can only feel good, wanted and valuable around such people right?

Not always! Here is the crux – if these individuals have the intelligence to work these skills in a positive manner, they also have the skill set to know exactly when and how to manipulate others into a false sense of security. Does this therefore mean that the leaders with higher Emotional Intelligence are also better liars or have a greater tendency to be less honest? I do not think that under normal circumstances this is the case.

But the very fact that they could use their skills and capabilities to bend the truth makes you think doesn't it? Have you experienced a leader who encourages you and builds you up only to let you down at the last minute, destroying your wishes and ambitions? Doesn't feel nice, does it? It feels like you have been used and questions your own reasons to be loyal. Let this be a small warning – be aware of those who pretend to be your "friends" or the best boss you ever had – they may speak with a forked tongue.

<hr>

Martin Luther King – An honest leader?

Who was he?

King was a clergyman, activist and the most prominent leader in the African-American civil rights campaigns in the 1960's. He is best known for his civil rights activities and non-violent civil disobedience. He has become a modern icon of civil rights not only in America but worldwide

What did he do?

"*I have a dream*" claimed King in what is today one of his most famous speeches delivered in Washington in 1963. This set the scene for him to become one of the greatest orators in US history, but it also built him a reputation as a radical and therefore placed him onto the radar of the FBI.

He won the Nobel Peace Prize in 1964 as a result of his non-violent approach to fight for racial equality. Later, his focus also shifted to poverty and the Vietnam War. He was assassinated in 1968, and since then has been posthumously awarded various commendations – even a US public holiday is named in memory of King.

What's interesting about him?

King was lucky to have been able to benefit from new technologies – namely the miracle of television in undertaking his work. This helped him reach more people and to be remembered as an inspirational speaker who's visionary and passionate speeches transformed the opinion of the population. He mobilised and unified people of all races and in doing so created an unprecedented bipartisan coalition for anti-racist legislation.

His nonviolent approach is probably the lynch pin to success – had he followed a course of violence the chances are, he and his followers would have been quickly and fatally suppressed. He was a charismatic and provocative public speaker as well as an emotional one.

He arguably spoke to and for African Americans and their mounting challenge to white oppression. When he died the non-violent movement seemed unable to continue without him and deepened the impression that he was its core and lifeblood – its great leader. His leadership, however, was often under close scrutiny.

Not everyone for example saw King as their icon for racial equality. King's charisma did not place him above criticism. Indeed, he was never able to gain mass support for his notion of nonviolent struggle as a way of life, rather many saw this no better than a simple tactic.

King's success as a leader was based on his intellectual and moral capabilities and his skill as a conciliator amongst movement activists who refused to be simply King's "followers" or "lieutenants".

Today, many argue that it was not King but rather the movement for racial equality that created the man – the man did not create the movement. The movement merely gave him a platform to voice his opinions and ideals. Certainly he was a critical element and his work should not be underestimated – but the civil rights movement should not be lost in the myth of one man.

Was he an honest leader?

There are some authors who now argue that he rejected aspects of the charismatic leader idea if they were in conflict with his own sense of moral limitations. He did not always demonstrate unwavering courage and was aware of his own limitations. For instance, when other colleagues once asked King to join them on the ride into Mississippi, he declined, saying: *"I think I should choose the time and place of my Golgotha"*.

I believe what makes King honest is not only his cause, but the way in which he went about achieving and promoting his beliefs. His non-violent approach and the "greater than me" objectives that aimed at correcting a social injustice make the man a martyr and his leadership good. Despite this, many referred to him as 'De Lawd' – and mistrusted a leader who preferred to cheer from the side lines.

Nevertheless, when asked about his own epitaph, he wanted to be remembered for giving his life to serve others, for trying to be right on the war question, for trying to feed the hungry and trying to cloth the naked. *"I want you to say that I tried to love and serve humanity."* Those aspects of King's life did not require charisma or other superhuman abilities. Just moral honesty.

Indeed, there are some cases of willful "misuse of power and intelligence". A perfect example of what can go wrong when executives choose to be less than honest can be found in the Lehman Brother's case, around the time of the beginning of the Financial Crisis in 2009. The Lehman Brothers mission statement from 2008:

"We are One Firm, defined by our unwavering commitment to our clients, our shareholders, and each other. Our vision is to build unrivalled partnerships with and value for our clients, through the knowledge, creativity, and dedication of our people, leading to superior results for our shareholders"

What happened? Despite having built up over $85 billion in mortgage backed securities the company filed for Chapter 11 bankruptcy protection (the largest in US history at the time) having debt totalling $619 billion. In essence the mortgage default crisis in 2007/2008 pushed the company over the edge – its exposure to the defaults was considerable. A court examiner found that the firms were using cosmetic accounting gimmicks to make the books appear less shaky than they really were. In fact the official report declared: *"a materially misleading picture of the firm's financial condition in late 2007 and 2008."* In other words, this was a blatant act of dishonesty. As I indicated earlier, stated intentions are often different to final actions.

But let's put the above into perspective – whilst intelligence can manipulate, people are fortunately still driven by moralistic thinking, so such examples whilst not uncommon are fortunately not yet the norm. Rather, there are many positives to those with high emotional intelligence, and their ability to drive innovative change, lead creative thinking, motivate and engage other people make these individuals highly sought after in the corporate world.

As a small diversion and by means of conclusion to our considerations on Emotional Intelligence and honesty, it is worth taking a quick peek into the world of mediation. This is a unique task that needs professionals who are able to balance truth, honesty, empathy and social skills. In essence, the mediator's role is to meet the emotional needs of each party in a conflict, such that truth (or a common concept of it) can be revealed and a conflict moved towards resolution. The mediator must by definition be a character who can display high levels of Emotional Intelligence.

Author Kenneth Cloke in his book "Mediating Dangerously" presents the mediation in a very enlightening manner. He argues that the mediation process is one integrated set of events, which allows *"the conflict to implode and explode without damaging the parties"*. The act of implosion is an increasing self-awareness and explosion the recognition of the problem that created conflict in the first place. The process is supported by deeply honest, empathetic questions that can defuse feelings and allow truth and positive feelings to flow.

In this explanation, we can immediately recognise aspects of Emotional Intelligence. It is the job of the mediator to model empathy, to focus on the real issues and help each party to *"grow into a part of themselves they have ignored or suppressed"*.

Cloke explains the necessity for honesty, given that each party to a conflict

- Holds a different view of the conflict, that is, who's to blame and why;

- Sees the world from the inside out, so empathy and honesty with the other is challenged, the ability to take responsibility is swept away and the need for support increased;
- Wears a mask to protect feelings of self-doubt or other deep emotions;
- Moves (intentionally) to self-protect against uncomfortable truths.

Indeed these arguments bring us back full loop to the points we considered when reviewing "truth". I argued that "pure truth" does not exist – we all have different beliefs and values as to what makes up truth. It is therefore up to the mediator to enter the conflict arena to *"model empathic listening, honest questioning, and equanimity in accepting painful answers"*.

So we have discovered that our level of Emotional Intelligence may be indicative of our intellectual capacity to lead others with more (or less) honesty. Perhaps the German philosopher Friedrich Nietzsche had a point 150 years ago when he suggested that those who refrain from lying do so only because of the difficulty involved in maintaining the lie. He believed that this supported his thought that we are divided according to strength and ability; thus, some of us tell the truth only out of (intellectual) weakness.

Or is it because we tell so many lies each day that we no longer have any awareness of us doing it? Is being honest a conscious decision at all?

DO WE KNOW WHEN WE ARE HONEST?

Some psychologists have spent many years constructing complex experiments to figure out how we play the moral game, how we decide when to cheat, lie, tell the whole truth or hide the rest. And the results have in some cases been surprising and more than a little concerning.

For years we have assumed that being honest is within our conscious control. Indeed many of the pages you have read until now argue that we know and understand what we are doing, when and why. We are fully aware that we are lying to protect, or lying to deceive and we are apparently happy to justify to ourselves why we manipulate numbers or lie to our employees.

But a study by Harvard's Joshua Greene and Joseph Paxton that measured brain activity at the time someone made a decision to lie has found some interesting results. They had wanted to see if the process that controls the desire to lie (a conscious process) was any different to that, which controlled the temptation to lie in the first place (an automatic process). They had hypothesised that if deciding to be honest is a conscious process – the result of resisting temptation – the areas of the brain associated with self-control and critical thinking would light up when subjects told the truth. If it is automatic, those areas would remain dark. In other words *"when we are honest, are we honest because we actively force ourselves to be? Or are we honest because it flows naturally?"* Greene asks.

What they found is that honesty *is* an automatic process – but only for some people. Comparing scans from tests of participants with and without the opportunity to cheat, the scientists found that for *already* honest subjects [pre-identified from a process of coin flipping used in their study], deciding to be honest took no extra brain activity.

Presumably therefore, the converse could also be true – that hypothetically, for already dishonest subjects, deciding to lie would also require no extra brain activity. If true, this is scary stuff, because it appears to support the idea that for some people at least, they are *not* consciously controlling their lying. They do not know they are being dishonest. Fortunately for those who do not have a pattern of either telling the truth or telling lies, the process of taking that decision required extra activity in the areas of the brain associated with critical thinking and self-control. In other words this needed conscious thought process.

Other studies, such as "the trolley problem", also demonstrate interesting results. In the original hypothesis of this older (1967) dilemma, the basic premise starts with the question as to whether one person can take an action, which may on one hand benefit some people but on the other hand harm others. For example, if a driver has lost control of a runaway trolley and has the choice to pick track A or track B and both are occupied with track workers, which track does he take? Either way, some people will die.

Can we, for example, do something with the intention to harm [lie] just because of a noble cause that sits behind this intention? Can you kill to save? Such questions challenge our "limits of morality" and many people will simply argue for what they believe is right in the context of the situation at the time, and thereafter "turn off" their moral radar and disengage from the whole thing.

Jon Haidt, a professor at the New York Stern School of Business and author of the Moral Foundation Theory, spent many years studying moral judgments and how people make decisions based on intuitions of what is "right and wrong". He discovered that we make some moral judgments based entirely on our emotions and are unable to explain logically why some things are right and others wrong. Does this include lying?

> "The decision to lie for personal gain turns out to be, at times, a strikingly unemotional choice"

Certainly the interesting point from some of these studies is that the decision to lie for personal gain turns out to be, at times, a strikingly unemotional choice. Some moral dilemmas like the trolley problem trigger emotional processing centres in our brains. In Greene's experiment above, there was no sign at all that emotions factored into a subject's decision to lie or to tell the truth. "Moral judgment is not a single thing", Greene concludes.

This may suggest that although we argue that "morality" is a guiding principle, our decision about what is right or wrong and subsequently deciding to tell the truth or to tell a lie may, in some situations, be an entirely separate process and not based upon what is morally correct.

If this is true, is it important to understand if we are capable of caring about honesty?

Do we care about being honest?

George Akerlof, in an article published in the American Economic review in the 1980's, suggested that *"the appearance of honesty is more beneficial"* and that *"there is a return to appearing honest, but not actually being honest"*. He even went so far as to state that we are willing to incur a cost to preserve this appearance.

Li Hao and D. Hausler further tested this in 2010. They published a paper entitled "true lies" that studied whether people actually preferred to *appear* honest but without actually *being* honest. They discovered that 95% of their test subjects were happy to incur a cost to maintain this appearance and once this appearance was established, people cheated to the greatest extent. In others words, if your boss is already lying, and all his peers and employees believe he is honest, there is a high chance he will continue to perpetuate this belief and make every effort to ensure his falsities go unnoticed.

How far will we go to maintain an honest appearance? Of course this is individually dependent, but take a peek at alibinetwork.com. On this site, for a fee, you can "buy" alibis and falsehoods such as airline confirmations, car rental receipts and hotel breaks, through to virtual "buddies", five day conference stays and fake jobs. In essence you can buy lies.

Duke University behavioural economist Dan Ariely argues in his book, "The Honest Truth about Dishonesty", that *"we lie to everyone, especially ourselves"*. Ariely blames our behaviours on two opposing motivations: We would like to view ourselves as honest, value-driven people, but we would also like to make as much money as possible or achieve other goals to get us ahead in life. Maybe therefore it pays to appear to be honest, but keep ourselves busy being dishonest.

In writing his book, Ariely spoke to insider traders and accountants who fudged financial statements, as well as consultants who padded their billable hours. *"One banker involved in insider trading told me he received all kinds of hints and secrets from his lawyer"*, Ariely said. *"He told himself it wasn't cheating since he wasn't getting precise tips and that everyone already had this information. It's all about rationalisation."*

The more we distance ourselves from the source of dishonesty, the less of a problem it becomes and the less we need to care. For example, most of us would never steal from the wallet of a singer – yet not hesitate to download the song at no cost. Further he argues that the less the chance of getting caught, the more likely we are to cheat.

As soon as we can argue "that everyone else is doing it", then we have justified our immoral actions to ourselves and will not stop. If everyone does it, why should I care? In this respect we find our earlier thread on moral disengagement is revisited, but this time it is not only about justifying a lie, it has now become the proliferation of a "don't care" attitude.

I think this is a danger sign and it worries me in terms of our search for honest leadership. If we know that more intelligent people may be able to better influence others and we also know that by disengaging from the consequences of a lie that we can begin the self-justification process, it potentially means that there are cold-hearted dishonest leaders out there that are knowingly manipulating others for personal gain. And they do not appear to care if they are prepared to buy lies from the likes of alibinetwork.com. If you also think this is a problem, then it is time to understand what a great leader should be.

THE SCENT IS LAID

We have reached the end of the first part of the walk. It's time to rest the dog, take a nap, eat and drink. So what have we discovered in the undergrowth and on our trail?

Do we understand honesty, or at least what it may be? I believe so. We have journeyed through morals, truth, lies and religion. We have considered attitude and intelligence and even our own awareness of honesty. We have discovered that some people are able to manipulate the truth, lie differently and still others are not even aware of when they are being honest or dishonest.

Probably the most important conclusion out of all these words however is that honesty starts with us. Our beliefs, morals, values, experiences, attitudes and opinions all contribute to our choosing to be or not to be honest. Only when you are honest to yourself, can you take the step to be more honest with others, specifically your followers.

However, before we ask how we could become more honest as a leader, we need to sow the seeds for the next part of the journey which involves ensuring that we have a common understanding of the tasks of leaders and what leadership actually is.

QUESTIONS FOR SELF-REFLECTION

We have reached the end of Part I. Important right now, however, is for you to reflect on what you have read. Below are a number of questions that you may wish to consider – can you answer them honestly and know why? Are you ready to be honest to yourself? Take these questions with you to your next dinner party or visit to the bar, and enjoy the conversation!

- Do I lie to myself?
- Do I believe religion to be honest? Why?
- Does the end justify the means?
- Is getting ahead more important than how I get there?
- Do I lie for personal gain, or retain information for myself?
- How trustworthy am I? Would others agree?
- Is it better to kill 10 to save 100?
- Am I aware of my lies, and if so, do I care?

PART II
SEARCHING FOR
LEADERSHIP

"The glue that holds all relationships together – including the relationship between the leader and the led is trust, and trust is based on integrity."
– Brian Tracy, author "How the best leaders lead"

"You can fool all the people some of the time, and some of the people all the time, but you cannot fool all the people all the time."
– Abraham Lincoln, US President 1861 – 1865

"My dog is usually pleased with what I do, because she is not infected with the concept of what I 'should' be doing."
– Lonzo Idolswine

Have you ever met an honest leader? If you have, what did he or she look like? What did they do, how did they speak, how did they behave? What motivated them? Doing the right thing? Or doing things right? Or simply being honest in whatever they did?

We have all met different leaders, be they your local priest, your boss, your kids sports team coach or even a local politician. Think about them and ask yourself why you remember them in particular. Is the memory a good one or a bad one? Why?

Take these few moments to ask yourself if they were always honest with you. Were they really open and authentic? When they did lie, did you know about it and did they care? Were these leaders good? Or did you just respect them because of their position as a leader or as your sports coach?

Often we come across people we believe to be honest, but they are not good leaders. Alternatively, we may interact with great leaders, but they are not always honest or do not always display the moral standing we would expect of a leader. So maybe we should be asking ourselves if the terms "leadership", "good" and "honesty" even fit together in one sentence or in today's society.

We all prefer to work or vote for honest leaders rather than dishonest ones. We also often hear that leaders should be the standard bearer of honesty and that we should come down hard on those who fail at it. But what does standard bearer mean? Does it mean we want our leaders to be more honest than us, which if true would imply that the rest of us – society – does not need to follow the same moral code. And if so, would this also not leave us susceptible to the risk that we end up with a leadership shortage as we cannot find anyone moral enough to fill the available leading positions? After all, there are not so many perfect leaders around as the regular political and business scandals demonstrate.

Or can we accept that it is OK for leaders to live by the same honest standards as the remainder of society? If the answer is yes, and considering the "public" role a leader inhabits, should we not be more diligent in sorting the wheat from the chafe and ensuring that rogue leaders cannot operate above the law, holding them more accountable for wrongdoings? This would ensure that society operates to the same common standard but at least our leaders, who theoretically are the "torch bearers" of our futures, are under more pressure to do the right things and not operate as if under some sense of special entitlement (as many do).

This is why we need to spend some time understanding what aspects of being a leader will engender honesty. We must not only consider leaders themselves, but also try to figure out why they do what they do, and why others choose to follow. Therefore this part of the journey will marry honesty and leadership together and in doing so, identify the traits that are likely to contribute to honest leadership and generate loyal followers.

THE NATURE OF THINGS

Since we lived in caves and figured out that Mother Nature has selected some of us to lead others, we have been asking questions in an effort to understand what makes leaders lead and followers follow. What makes them who they are? And why should we trust our leaders anyway?

Joanne Ciulla, in Chapter 13 of the book "The Nature of Leadership" argues that the study of honesty, when combined with the ideas about leadership styles and practices, has tended to present two overlapping questions.

The first is *"what is a leader?"* The earliest answers to this question evolved in the 1920's with the advent of the so called "Great man theories" and "Trait theories" (leaders are born), and later evolved into "behavioural theories" (leadership can be taught). These initial ideas have ballooned over the subsequent decades such that today several generic leadership theories exist. The mind map below provides a quick overview of the key "branches" of thought that have evolved over time:

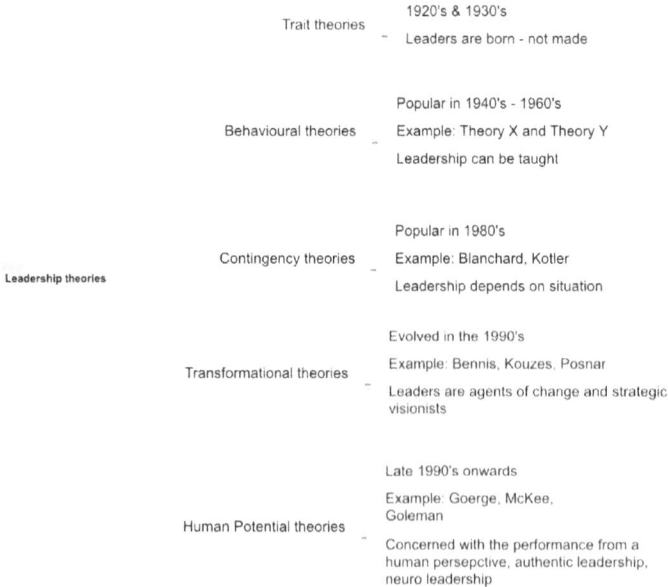

| Trait theories | 1920's & 1930's |
| | Leaders are born - not made |

Behavioural theories	Popular in 1940's - 1960's
	Example: Theory X and Theory Y
	Leadership can be taught

Contingency theories	Popular in 1980's
	Example: Blanchard, Kotler
	Leadership depends on situation

Leadership theories

Transformational theories	Evolved in the 1990's
	Example: Bennis, Kouzes, Posnar
	Leaders are agents of change and strategic visionists

Human Potential theories	Late 1990's onwards
	Example: Goerge, McKee, Goleman
	Concerned with the performance from a human persepctive, authentic leadership, neuro leadership

Within each you can find a plethora of models visualised in triangles, circles, pyramids and squares that break down the characteristics of leaders. Many of these models support different ideas about leaders and their capabilities. You should take your pick. It's easy to find one model that you like and focus on it if you believe this is who you want to be.

The problem, notes Ciulla, is that many of these popular theories confuse the actual to the ideal when it comes to describing the traits of leaders. Often we will read terms that describe leaders as being visionary, trustworthy, authentic, bold, curious and so on. But all too often these descriptions of leaders are not reflective of *who they are*, rather they are based on societies expectations of what a leader *ought to be*. And as we know, most leaders do not live up to these standards.

Being able to answer the question "what a leader is" leads naturally onto the second and more challenging question posed by Ciulla: "*What is good leadership?*" And the answer to this depends on our individual understanding of the first question, which also means that subsequent thinking starts to become more philosophical.

"Leaders do not command excellence, they have to earn it"

What for instance, do we understand by the term "good", when we refer to leadership? Do we mean good in terms of getting things done (productive), or do we refer to good as doing the right things (driven by honesty and morality)? I agree with writers who argue that finding one leader who can do both (productive and moral) at the same time is nigh on impossible. We rarely find many examples of great leaders who are both effective and ethical; even popular leaders such as Steve Jobs or many of the others I refer to in these pages display a mean streak and questionable moral judgement in their pursuit of great things.

We must also accept that leaders do not command excellence, they have to earn it. Excellence is a big word and could in this respect be defined as "be all you can be". Presumably, to "be all you can be" leaders must be able to recognise all that they are and in turn have the courage to take the steps needed to plug any gap between who they are and all they can be. They must find the personal drive to become a top dog. John F Kennedy said *"Courage – not complacency – is our need today. Leadership not salesmanship"*.

Followers do not wait around or make plans to achieve certain goals and just hope that their leaders can fulfil them. If you are a leader and think like this, may I suggest you update your ideas? This type of thinking is backwards. We all rightly expect our leaders to understand that pursuing excellence is not the same as accomplishing a job or task.

Rather leadership excellence is about looking after the goals of the followers, not the leaders themselves, through pursuing courage, the development of self-awareness, understanding personal limitations and finding the strength to inspire and motivate others. If a political leader does not look after their constituents, they are not representing the values that they espoused when voted – and this is dishonest.

Therefore, to make progress for our purposes we need to not only take a step back, but also must delve deeper into these questions of leader and leadership. To assist me in this I have borrowed the ideas from acknowledged leadership experts such as Daniel Goleman and Warren Bennis. Also, if this fascinates you I recommend you read more about leadership focussing specifically on transformational and human potential theories by authors such as James Kouzes & Barry Posner, Robert Kelly, Bill George and Annie McKee to name a few.

Bearing in mind this is the 21st century I will take the liberty to dismiss the idea that leaders are born and leadership positions should be inherited. Also, I disagree that leadership cannot be somehow learned because we are by nature (at least the intelligent ones amongst us) able to learn from our mistakes. In doing this we become more effective at doing what we do. Even dogs can figure out that they get no bone when they keep making the same mistake. Some of us are better at it than others, and that may be down to genes, but ultimately we are taught (or copy and improve) many of things that we know and skills that we have.

LEADERS – DEALERS IN TRUST

According to the Oxford English Dictionary a leader is *"a guiding or directing head, as of an army, movement or political group".* But additional definitions also refer to a leader as a (British) newspaper article, a musical composer, the lead violinist in an orchestra or the shoot of a plant!

And for leadership: *"The activity of leading a group of people or an organisation or the ability to do this".* There are many similar definitions to be found but common to all is the idea that leaders are individuals who, by their actions, facilitate the movement of a group of people toward a common or shared goal.

But Warren Bennis, an American Scholar, organisation consultant and generally seen as one of the "founding fathers" behind many leadership theories argues that is it not that simple. He stated: *"I used to think that running an organisation was equivalent to conducting a symphony orchestra. But I don't think that's quite it; it's more like jazz. There is more improvisation".* And herein lies the challenge as there is no one singular definition which particularly stands out or is agreed upon for both "leader" and "leadership". All are inspiring or motivating depending on your own opinion. Some of those I particularly enjoy:

"A leader is a dealer in hope."
– Napoleon

"If your actions inspire others to dream more, learn more, do more and become more, you are a leader."
– John Quincy Adams (US President 1825 – 1829)

"A leader is best when people barely know he exists, when his work is done, his aim fulfilled, they will say: we did it ourselves."
– Lao Tzu (ancient Chinese philosopher)

"The quality of a leader is reflected in the standards they set for themselves."
– Ray Kroc (Founder of McDonalds)

"It is better to lead from behind and to put others in front, especially when you celebrate victory when nice things occur. You take the front line when there is danger. Then people will appreciate your leadership."
– Nelson Mandela (President South Africa 1994 – 1999 and racial equality activist)

"Leadership is a function of knowing yourself, having a vision that is well communicated, building trust among colleagues and taking effective action to realise your own leadership potential."
– Warren Bennis (Leadership scholar)

"When there is no vision, the people perish."
– Proverbs 29:18

"Leadership is practiced not so much in words as in attitude and in actions."
– Harold Geneen (Business person & President of ITT, the Telephone and Telegraph Corporation)

"The task of the leader is to get his people from where they are to where they have not been."
– Henry Kissinger (writer, political scientist, diplomat)

Many of these imply that leadership is an influence process. The distinction between leader and leadership is important, but potentially confusing. In simple terms the leader is an individual; leadership is the function, process or activity this individual performs.

I prefer to argue that great leadership is similar to being a chef in a restaurant. A chef takes all the ingredients given to him and with the aid of his own knowledge, experience, skills and perhaps a portion of luck will mix these together to create the perfect tasty dinner. Or of course, if he is still trying to learn the ropes he may make a complete hash up and produce the worst dinner you have ever had the misfortune to eat!

And just like leaders in organisations, in politics or in sports, different chefs will be more or less successful with the same ingredients, depending upon how their experiences, values, education and culture have taught them to mix these ingredients together. At the end of the day we all will use different methods with the same ingredients to achieve similar goals.

The important thing for me however, is not to spend time understanding what they have achieved; rather it is more interesting to realise *how* they have achieved it. And herein can be found the roots of honest leadership – a leader cannot be let off the moral hook if they achieve their goals using immoral methods – even at times if their cause is just. They are in the public eye and must set the moral standards – "walk the talk" for the rest of us to follow.

Margaret Thatcher – An honest leader?

Who was she?

Margaret Thatcher was the UK Secretary of State for Education from 1970 – 1975 and became head of the British right wing Conservative Party from 1975. In this role she held the post of Prime Minister from 1979 – 1990, making her the longest serving Prime Minister in the 20th century. She was also notable as being the first women to hold this most senior political position in the UK.

What did she do?

She was primarily responsible for the development of monetarist economic thinking in the UK, lowering inflation in her first 3 years from 18% to just over 8% and improving UK GDP by 23% in 10 years. She introduced policies to restrict the money supply, lower direct taxes, increase indirect taxes and most especially instigated large scale deregulation of state owned companies in the 1980's.

In doing so she broke the back of powerful trade unions that had held sway over "business" in its drive for labour productivity. During her time she increased the number of adults owning shares in public companies from 7% to 25% and encouraged more than a million occupiers of rented "council homes" to buy their own properties. Personal wealth increased by 80%.

In 1982 she rallied the nation behind a war and subsequent victory against Argentina over the disputed Falkland Islands, helping to secure a second election win in 1983.

What's interesting about her?

She was a lady of uncompromising character, holding the toughest political job in the country and operating within a traditional male dominated world. She possessed a remarkable ability to articulate her views of morality and vision. Upon coming to power in 1979, she said: *"Where there is discord, may we bring harmony. Where there is error, may we bring truth. Where there is doubt, may we bring faith. And where there is despair, may we bring hope"*.

However, despite these emotional speeches, she was a dominating, competitive and often confrontational leader. Since her resignation in the 1990's, curiosity about her legacy has increased, culminating in a movie, "The Iron Lady", being released in 2012. She inherited this term in 1976 from the Soviets as a result of her opposition to communism. And it is a fitting term – her very presence would strike fear into the hearts of many, from fellow world leaders to the "tory wets" she brutally purged from her cabinet.

Her political ideology of monetarism, privatisation and self-help was termed "Thatcherism", and today this vision of social and economic order has become a focal point of many political scientists. But it is also seen as a reflection of Thatcher herself – her personal toughness and her belief that with determined self-confidence the vanguard will always "win through".

It is argued by some that during her time as Britain's leader she managed to transform not just one political party but two. By the time the opposition Labour Party regained power after an absence from it of more than 20 years, Thatcherism was so engrained into British society that it became an accepted and irreversible fact.

Was she an honest leader?

On the one hand Thatcher can be considered to be a transformational and charismatic leader, who worked towards a higher level of morality by communicating clear visions and road maps to achieve it. She was open and clear about her beliefs and from the earliest days in office clarified her intentions to transform the UK: *"Unless we change our ways and our direction, our greatness as a nation will soon be a footnote in the history books, a distant memory of an offshore island, lost in the mists of time like Camelot, remembered kindly for its noble past"*. This was Thatcher's version of the truth.

On the other hand, there are some who would argue she was directive, militant and authoritarian. She certainly demonstrated certain traits such as aggressiveness, self-confidence, dominance and a strong moral belief of how things should be. Thatcher has said: *"I am extraordinarily patient, provided I get my own way in the end"*. Also "*I don't mind how much my Ministers talk, so long as they do what I say*", or "*I shan't be pulling the levers... but I shall be a very good back-seat driver*". In this respect her Cabinet was frequently cleaned out and dissenting personalities were often publicly removed. It could be argued her leadership approach was not honest – it did not always generate loyalty and trust in the same manner an ethical, visionary and participative leader should be able to do.

Nevertheless for 20 years the majority of the British public accepted her vision of the truth. Presumably your final beliefs will depend not only upon your political tendencies but also for many readers your own personal experiences and memories of her policies. Whatever your view, as a leader she left a lasting legacy.

Therefore, I believe that to inspire and motivate others, leadership becomes a process of applying knowledge and skills to influence potential followers. Indeed this thinking was originally called process leadership – but we also know today that leadership is not that simple. Just as our Chef uses experience, personal taste and opinions in preparing his recipe, the process of applying knowledge and skills will be influenced by a leader's character, beliefs, morals and attitudes – the so called traits.

It is these traits, specifically honesty and trust, which is fundamental to being a leader and inspired Warren Bennis in his book "On becoming a leader" to write "*It became clear that the ability to inspire trust, not charisma, is what enables leaders to recruit others to a cause.*"

In an article in Leadership Excellence magazine, Bennis refers to Jim Burke, CEO of Johnson & Johnson (J&J), who, in 1982, boldly recalled at a cost of $100 million all Tylenol nationwide because some poisoned pills had been discovered. His candour and openness by personally going on national television to announce the recall was unprecedented at the time, and it is at least partly responsible for saving the brand equity of the organisation.

In my view this is a perfect example of leaders "doing the right thing", and in this instance the remarkable aspect is that sales of Tylenol actually increased because of the ethical handling of the situation.

Bennis continues to argue that a leader is by definition an innovator. They do things other people haven't done or don't do. They do things in advance of other people. They make new things and make old things new. They embrace risks and mistakes, learning from adversity. They reflect on all of their experiences. In other words they become more self-aware and honest with themselves, which as we know is reflective of Goleman's Emotional Intelligence model.

If trust is to be built, then our leaders must recognise and understand within their leadership process how others around them feel. And this understanding must come from "within"- the head and the heart. For example, if a leader becomes aware that being dishonest poisons the atmosphere and appears to lead to a lack of performance, we should be able to expect them to correct their ways. This means that a motivator for being honest must be empathy. The moral compass of a leader, to "do the right things" is underpinned by social responsibility, which also has foundations within Emotional Intelligence.

Bennis argues that leaders do not seek to lead. Instead, they seek to express themselves fully and in doing that inspire others to follow. Leadership is a "way of being". You have to be motivational, visionary and inspirational. But you cannot just "do" visionary, or "do" motivational. You have to live it. This, I believe, is the heart of leadership that many leaders must still discover.

> *"Leaders do not seek to lead, they seek to express themselves fully and in doing that inspire others to follow"*

The success of the leadership process – the ability to influence others – is in part dependent upon a leader being honest and empathetic. But the debate is not over. The problem is that we judge good leadership as an effective process that can bring about change, and this ends up creating a split between doing ethical things and being ethical as an individual. We end up being intellectually stimulated by great leaders such as Adolf Hitler, but morally disgusted by what he did.

But before we go further we must also discuss the issue of management. Many professionals argue that management is about handling complexity to create order and a sense of predictability, whereas leadership is about promoting change. Clear is that an organisation needs both, leaders and managers to survive and to promote organisational effectiveness.

But is there a difference? I can imagine that some of you with "manager" in your job title may begin to wonder if you are also a leader. Honest leadership sounds good. So what about managers? After all, many managers have teams of people to direct and instruct right?

If I am a manager, am I a leader?

Before we go ahead and consider this, let's take a quick test. Grab a pen and paper and answer the following. Then take a look at the answer key for a brief discussion of each question.

1. TRUE or FALSE: I think more about immediate results than I do about mentoring others.

2. TRUE or FALSE: People will be motivated if you pay them enough.

3. TRUE or FALSE: It's nice to know about people's long-term goals, but not necessary to get the job done.

4. TRUE or FALSE: If you have a consistent recognition system that rewards everyone in the same way, then that is enough.

5. TRUE or FALSE: The best way to build a team is to set a group goal that is highly challenging, maybe even "crazy".

6. TRUE or FALSE: My greatest pleasure in my job comes from making the work process more effective.

7. TRUE or FALSE: I spend more of my time and attention on my weaker performers than I do on my top performers, who basically take care of themselves.

8. TRUE or FALSE: It's better not to know anything about the personal lives and interests of the people who report to me.

9. TRUE or FALSE: Sometimes, it's almost as if I'm a "collector of people" because I'm always recruiting and getting to know new people.

10. TRUE or FALSE: I like to surround myself with people who are better at what they do than I am.

11. TRUE or FALSE: People talk about "mission" too much – it's best just to let people do their work and not try to bring values into the conversation.

12. TRUE or FALSE: It's my job to know everything that goes on in my area.

13. TRUE or FALSE: I pay close attention to how and where I spend my time, because the priorities I put into action are the ones that other people will observe and follow.

Done? Here are the answers, and a few words to each.

1. TRUE or FALSE: I think more about immediate results than I do about mentoring others. Managers focus on the process and immediate efficiency more than leaders do. Leaders think about how they invest their time to develop the strongest talent so that their best followers can grow and do more over time. Leaders figure if they do that, their best performers will do a better job of watching and improving processes than they themselves will. "True" is more of a manager's response, and "False" is more of a leader's response.

2. TRUE or FALSE: People will be motivated if you pay them enough. Leaders understand that financial reward keeps us happy, but it is not a true motivator. Once our salary is at an acceptable level, we tend to be more motivated by the nature of the work, by the challenges and opportunities from which we can learn and grow, and based on whether or not we feel our bosses support us or care about us. "True" is more of a manager's response, and "False" is more of a leader's response.

3. TRUE or FALSE: It's nice to know about people's long-term goals, but not necessary to get the job done. Remember the quote from Mr. Kissinger earlier? Leaders take us to places we have not yet been. To do this, they need to know about our long-term goals and aspirations, so they can craft ways to combine our personal goals with the work at hand. For a given project, it may be less important to know our long-term goals, but for organisational success and growth it is necessary. "True" is more of a manager's response, and "False" is more of a leader's response.

4. TRUE or FALSE: If you have a consistent recognition system that rewards everyone in the same way, then that is enough. Leaders' recognise that we are all differently motivated, meaning the same recognition system will not be a panacea for all. Some of us like public praise whilst some of us prefer the opportunity to have flexible family time. Leaders can recognise this and "flex" their approach to us accordingly. Since managers emphasise systems more than they do people or personalities, "True" is more of a manager's response, and "False" is more of a leader's response.

5. TRUE or FALSE: The best way to build a team is to set a group goal that is highly challenging, maybe even "crazy". Manager's tend to think more in terms of what has been done before and try to make more incremental improvements, while leaders like to challenge us to bring out our best in ways we may not have imagined possible. The best way to build team coherence is to take people through a shared, difficult challenge – something any military platoon leader can tell you. "True" is more of a leader's response, and "False" is more of a manager's response.

6. TRUE or FALSE: My greatest pleasure in my job comes from making the work process more effective. This is a classic manager's priority, deriving most pleasure from process and efficiency. Leaders enjoy that a lot too, but they tend to enjoy most when they can help followers and organisations grow. "True" is more of a manager's response, and "False" is more of a leader's response.

7. TRUE or FALSE: I spend more of my time and attention on my weaker performers than I do on my top performers, who basically take care of themselves. Leaders use their time as a reward and seek to invest their attention where it can have the most upside impact. Generally speaking, we have the most opportunity to grow in areas where we have already demonstrated strong performance, and so leaders tend to avoid remedial projects or the constant oversight of weaker performers.

Instead, they spend more of their attention on those of us who are the best at what we do since this group represents those who will bring the greatest process and performance improvements in the future. Managers tend to focus more on problems to solve than they do on opportunities to boost their team towards previously unachieved levels of excellence. "True" is more of a manager's response, and "False" is more of a leader's response.

8. TRUE or FALSE: It's better not to know anything about the personal lives and interests of the people who report to me. Leaders try to learn what makes each of us tick, which means getting to know us personally but with being invasive or inappropriate. Managers tend to be more cut-and-dried in their work relations. "True" is more of a manager's response, while "False" is more of a leader's response.

9. TRUE or FALSE: Sometimes, it's almost as if I'm a "collector of people" because I'm always recruiting and getting to know new people. Some of the best managers are very good at studying best practices – ways to "build a better mousetrap" to improve performance and efficiency. Leaders tend to look more for the star performers of the world who are more likely to invent those better mousetraps in the first place. Leaders think about their teams and their talents as if they were investment opportunities, and so "True" is more of a leader's response, and "False" is more of a manager's response

10. TRUE or FALSE: I like to surround myself with people who are better at what they do than I am. This is a classic leadership statement, since leaders are all about finding and cultivating talent and are not threatened by it. Managers may tend to want to feel more in control of their surroundings – not least of all because highly talented people can be very independent and difficult to "manage"! Since leaders tend to have stronger social skills than managers do and so are better prepared to deal with other strong egos, "True" is more of a leader's response, and "False" is more of a manager's response.

11. TRUE or FALSE: People talk about "mission" too much – it's best just to let people do their work and not try to bring values into the conversation. While it's true that "mission" and "vision" are concepts that have become watered down by careless misuse, leaders still understand that it is best to connect daily work and projects into a larger framework that gives our work a sense of purpose and meaning. Most of us would rather feel that our work adds value which enables us to work well and care about results. "True" is more of a manager's response, and "False" is more of a leader's response.

12. TRUE or FALSE: It's my job to know everything that goes on in my area. Since leaders focus more on knowing those of us who know what is going on, rather than on the details of everything that is going on, "True" is more of a manager's response, and "False" is more of a leader's response.

13. TRUE or FALSE: I pay close attention to how and where I spend my time, because the priorities I put into action are the ones that other people will observe and follow. Leaders realise that the little things they do ripple out and have far reaching effects. As a result, they make their choices wisely, knowing that followers and other managers or supervisors do imitate the "boss", who sets the ultimate tone. "True" is more of a leader's response, and "false" is more of a manager's response.

So what have we learned? Are managers the same as leaders? In short, no – managers are not leaders and leaders are somehow more than managers. As Peter Drucker stated *"Managers do things right; leaders do the right things".* Further, Warren Bennis wrote *"The manager asks how and when; the leader asks what and why".*

Leadership and management are often confused with one another. Many keyboards have been worn out writing about these differences. The manager's job is to plan, organise and coordinate. The leader's job is to inspire and motivate. In his 1989 book "On Becoming a Leader", Warren Bennis composed a list of the differences that I have extracted directly for their relevance:

- The manager administers; the leader innovates.
- The manager is a copy; the leader is an original.
- The manager maintains; the leader develops.
- The manager focuses on systems and structure; the leader focuses on people.
- The manager relies on control; the leader inspires trust.
- The manager has a short-range view; the leader has a long-range perspective.
- The manager asks how and when; the leader asks what and why.
- The manager has his or her eye always on the bottom line; the leader's eye is on the horizon.
- The manager imitates; the leader originates.
- The manager accepts the status quo; the leader challenges it.
- The manager is the classic good soldier; the leader is his or her own person.
- The manager does things right; the leader does the right thing.

Leadership is therefore much more about behaviour rather than processes. Good leaders are followed chiefly because people trust and respect them, rather than any pure "technical" skills they may possess. If we return for a moment to our book metaphor, we quickly discover that some dogs are more like leaders – they inspire and motivate us: blind dogs, rescue dogs, police dogs to name but a few, have all been trained to do great things.

Management relies heavily on tangible measurable capabilities such as effective planning, the use of organisational systems and the use of appropriate communication methods. In contrast, leadership involves many management skills, but generally as a secondary function of true leadership.

Leadership instead tends to focus on the "squishy and soft" stuff that many of us shy away from, such as trust, inspiration, attitude, vision, decision-making and personal character. These things may not be the result of experience, but many would argue are moral facets of humanity and often come combined with a high Emotional Intelligence and self-awareness.

This does not necessarily mean that leaders cannot be good managers or organisations that have more managers than capable leaders are worse off than those with more leaders. It always depends on the functions that are held and the purpose for which we are employed. It's pretty pointless for example, if an organisation employs a "manager" to motivate the global workforce behind the newly defined vision & values of a multi-national company. The manager is more likely to be used to following orders, organising the work, assigning the right people to the necessary tasks, coordinating the results and ensuring the job gets done as ordered – it's therefore highly probable that the manager will be quickly out of his depth. Their focus is on efficiency not vision.

Equally, employing a highly skilled leader to ensure that boxes are packed on a production line is a waste of talent and skill and will probably end in tears. Leadership and management must go hand in hand. They are not the same thing. But they are necessarily linked, and complementary. Every company needs both, managers to keep things running efficiently and leaders to work out how to keep the order books filled in the first place. Any effort to separate the two is likely to cause more problems than it solves, and every organisation needs its fair share of both, managers and leaders.

Critical is that any leader should know that the word "team" has no "i". Leaders should know that trust overcomes all common egos and is at the heart of a great team. Skilful leaders build teams on trust, with a dash of respect.

> *"Leaders should know that trust overcomes all common egos and is at the heart of a great team"*

One of the ways they do this is by engendering feelings of belonging or connectedness and breaking down the silos that inhibit communication. By implication they work on relationships and not just numbers and facts. They can transform the climate around them by having faith in their followers and by acting in such a way that teammates can rely on the leaders' promises.

According to a study by the Hay Group (Lamb & Mckee 2004), a global management consultancy, there are 75 key components of employee satisfaction. They found that trust and confidence in top leadership was the single most reliable predictor of employee satisfaction in an organisation. Effective communication by leadership in three critical areas was the key to winning our trust and confidence:

1. Helping us understand the company's overall business strategy.
2. Helping us understand how we contribute to achieving that strategy.
3. Sharing information with us on both how the company is doing and how our own division is doing – relative to strategic business objectives.

We all want to be guided by leaders we can respect and who have a clear sense of direction. To gain that respect, our leaders must be truthful and honest and not just act like a manager imparting instruction and direction. But is this enough for us to follow our leaders?

FOLLOWERS OR LEMMINGS

We frequently use the lemming metaphor to refer to those who have blind faith in their leaders and follow them somewhat over zealously down every path. They jump when their leader asks, do what their leader does, believe what their leader believes and like a lemming would probably go over the end of a cliff if that's where their leader led.

I cannot help but be disturbed by the naivety of these followers and the incredible self-righteousness of the leaders who have become over passionate about their moral correctness. They unfairly use their intelligence and influential skills to exploit the trust of others often with disastrous outcomes for all concerned.

The most extreme examples we can find are perhaps best found within a religious cult. For example, in the 1990s in Waco in Texas a gun battle and siege began between David Koresh, the leader of the Branch Davidian cult, its 70 or so followers and the FBI. The standoff ended the lives of most of the cult followers in a tragic fire. The point is, the members of the cult did not surrender and stayed put supporting Koresh until the very end. Were they lemmings? No, not in the literal sense, but why did they follow Koresh? Why do millions follow the preaching's of The Pope? Why do we all vote for our political leaders? Why do we all stay for many hours every day in our jobs if we are not energised or motivated in the daily function?

Are all followers really lemmings? No, the majority are not. Maybe they follow because of hope? Well, according to Napoleon we know that he believed a leader is a dealer in hope.

But Napoleon may also have noticed that he could not just stand at the front of the army, yell 'charge' and then run forward. He may have been surprised when his army did not always follow. And yet, many would-be leaders do just this. They think they can be leaders just by telling people to follow them. They believe their power, position and authority would be reason enough to be obeyed. But then they are surprised when their followers do not follow or only half a job gets done by the de-motivated few who decide to obey.

Benjamin Hoff, a US author said *"Lots of people talk to dogs…. Not very many listen, though…. That's the problem"*. Remember, dogs do not follow when they do not trust and I cannot help but wonder if new leaders should not first learn to work with dogs before they are let loose on people! Failing with the dog would be a sign to leaders that they need to change their approach, as people are just the same. People may follow out of fear, but not respect. And because many followers are not lemmings, lasting followship needs more than position, power and authority.

And this is sometimes a challenge for leaders. They are not always the top dogs they like to think they are because followers are seldom blind. They pay attention to their leaders' actions and behaviours. And will then decide for themselves how and when to respond. Thus, leaders often get trapped in the so-called "leadership-follower-loop". Think about it – leaders do their daily job and lead. And each follower will gossip. They gossip all the time. They gossip online in social media sites such as twitter and Facebook and offline at home, or at a friend's house or even in the workplace restaurant. Sometimes they gossip about the work, sometimes about colleagues and many times about their leaders.

Followers invariably talk amongst themselves if their leader does something that concerns them. And they do this long before their leaders discover what is happening. I am sure that the leaders amongst you will be well aware of this, or have at least a nagging suspicion "you" or your actions are being discussed behind your back – why else does all go quiet the minute you walk into the area where your team is seated?

The leader and the organisations around them must be sensitive to this and adjust their behaviours accordingly. If they do not, just as some people may stay if their leaders get it right, then the many of us who are voluntarily following our leaders will also abandon in droves if they get it wrong. Be realistic: if a better deal can be found elsewhere, and followers remain unconvinced about their leaders and their behaviours, they will have every reason to move on.

Let's be honest – how many leaders and organisations do you know with high employee turnover? Employers often feed the same "external influences" excuses (salaries, market place opportunities and so on) as to why so many people leave their organisation. But the fact is 50% of all leavers do so because of the boss – not external influences. But how many organisations deal with bad bosses? If they are effective at achieving targets, regardless of *how* they are achieved, they get to stay. Is that morally right? Of course not.

Bright leaders and clever forward thinking organisations will at some point realise this and begin to self-diagnose what is happening, maybe ask open questions or think about more intense leadership development. But this must work across *all* levels of leadership, not just the few. And this diagnostic process must go deep into the organisational heart and operate as a continual sanity check.

Many organisations over the years have developed a specific set of leadership behaviours against which leaders are measured and their development plans identified. This is a good start towards honest leadership – but it is not enough. The trouble, I believe, is that too many organisations assume that this relatively simple action is a panacea – introduce a new set of "ideal" behaviours, follow with a little training and "hey presto", our leaders are perfect and our problems are solved!

But this does not happen. In part because the pre-specified behaviours are simply not robust enough. They may have been developed internally (by asking for example existing leaders – presumably good ones – what they believe makes a great leader), and they are sometimes not backed up with sufficient benchmarking.

This means that there is a risk the behaviours become "inward" looking, in that they align to the *current* state of the organisation and less so the *future desired* direction. The intentions behind the behaviours can also be diluted because they may end up being heavily based upon internal, often top down assumptions about what is "right" or "wrong".

Also, many organisations struggle to develop leadership behaviours that are flexible enough for culturally diverse entities. Even benchmarking should be carefully considered to ensure that it includes organisations in all key markets where the behaviours are intended to be integrated. Poorly defined global "standards" may result in some leaders being unable to relate to the stated behaviours of an organisation and dismiss them out of hand. Perhaps even more concerning, it is not unusual for such behavioural frameworks to be specified without any input from the very people who should benefit in the first instance!

Surely, wouldn't it be better to try to understand the expectations of the followers being led (what makes them stay, what would make them leave) or the customers who are buying (what's great, not so great) and combine this input with that from (global) benchmarking and internal leadership? Would this not give a different picture of leadership expectations rather than referring only to the existing leaders themselves? I believe it would.

Assuming the leader and organisation can get this far, subsequent development for the leaders should be compulsory and continuous if the behaviours are to be "lived". With a set of well-defined behaviours that are trained and implemented, we introduce a closed leader-follower system, where followers respond to leaders and they in turn respond to followers. We are therefore engaged in an on-going dance, a dynamic interplay in which followers and leaders closely monitor one another and respond accordingly.

This is important, because when followers are deciding if they respect their leaders, they do not think about their attributes, but rather observe what their leaders do and say (as much as what is not done or said) to work out who they really are. Followers will try to understand if their leaders are honourable, live by their promises, walk the talk and ultimately if they can be trusted.

Jack Welch says that earning this trust is enormously powerful in an organisation. Without it, people will not do their best. Warren Bennis calls it the major leadership challenge of today and tomorrow. Why is trust so important? At the end of the day we spend too many years of our lives slaving away at our jobs – for our companies, the customers and of course our boss and the bosses boss. If we cannot trust our leader who is allegedly guiding us, then how can we trust them to do the right thing for us and stand by us when needed?

But is trust the only reason we follow leaders? At the end of the day leaders are not leaders if they do not have followers. And followers follow for more reasons than just trust in a leader. We must remember that people don't just follow anyone. We can't just say 'follow me' and expect people to follow out of the goodness of their hearts.

Followers are in some cases *paid* to follow. In these instances they are, in essence, prostituting their time. But even prostitutes like to be happy! Others amongst us follow because following happens to meet our personal objectives and the leader helps us fulfil them. Followers need leaders and leaders need followers.

So let's turn the coin over from leadership and instead think about "followship". This term was summarised nicely by the 19th century British Prime Minister Benjamin Disraeli, who said: *"I must follow the people. Am I not their leader?"*. It is believed he said this as an ironic comment, referring to his belief that as an elected leader, it is the wishes of the people he must follow, not his wishes they must follow.

Followship recognises that it is not only leaders who have emotions and influences, but also followers. They have a role with a specialised set of skills, motivations and the power to enhance organisational potential. Followers may follow for reasons other than just trust, such as:

Fear of retribution: *"If I do not follow, I may lose my job!"* Fear is a strong reason to follow. But this is not following. This is akin to having teeth pulled without an anaesthetic. Invariably the leader is being directive and abusive, either because they have no choice or know no other way. Fear is not the tool of effective leaders (and certainly not ethical leaders). At best, fear-based approaches gain weak commitment and need constant attention should the follower freeze or flee.

Friendship & blind admiration: *"I've followed him around for years and will always do so"*. Oh dear. It seems that our follower is a lemming. Can the leader really do no wrong? This is not loyalty – it's blind admiration. Maybe it has happened because the follower feels respected; maybe they believe they owe the leader a favour; maybe they believe that their package is great; maybe they are sleeping with the boss (and have a fear of retribution). We probably will never know. But the obvious risk here is that other team members can see this follower as the "teacher's pet" and it may create resentment. Also, the follower may never grow to be something more as they always agree with the leader and they are unable to see a different perspective. Either way they become "yes" people.

Hope: *"We must do something. I hope this works!"* This is the hope based follower that Napoleon would love. Here the leader is trading in the fact that hope dies last and maybe we will all be OK if we stick together. The risk of course is that many of us who see a different reality may well jump ship. Maybe the follower's truth is different to that of the leader – the leader must find other ways of inspiring and motivating.

Intellectual or common agreement: *"What a good idea. That makes real sense."* Educated people often like reasons and logical explanations. If it makes sense or is somehow aligned to our thinking, the leader will encourage followship because of the common intellect and approach. It often needs a leader to encourage a team to collectively buy into an idea.

Buying into the vision: *"What a brilliant idea. Let me be a part of it."* This kind of followship is similar to the above but centres around emotion – we respond to the visionary capability of a leader to sell an idea. We do not follow the leader, but the emotion and passion for an ideal. Visionary leaders are often revered and wanted as they are effective at inspiring and motivating us. However, the approach must be sustained over a period of time. It is one thing to have a vision and it is another to keep going during the difficult days of implementation.

Steve Jobs – An honest leader?

Who was he?

Steve Jobs is the main man behind Apple. Having co-founded it in 1976 and getting kicked out in 1985, he returned 12 years later to rescue the organisation from near bankruptcy. Today, Apple is the world's most valuable company, a distinction it had earned by the time he died at the end of 2011.

What did he do?

He effectively helped revolutionise and in doing so mobilise the world of music and communication. Beginning with the first digital music player, the iPod and the iTunes music store, he quickly followed with the iPhone and iPad. Together, these devices have collectively transformed the face of several industries including music, photography, retailing, publishing, movies and computing. The basic act of human contact is becoming a virtual event.

Job's is considered by some to be the creator of an organisation that today sells over 156 million mobile devices per year and purports a market capitalisation that is 17 times greater than Ford, worth more than the amount spent on two Apollo space programmes, roughly equal to 300 years of business for Irish beer producers and exceeds the GDP of countries such as Belgium, Poland and Sweden. Wow!

What's interesting about him?

Jobs had a remarkable capability to mix entrepreneurship and imagination with technology and business. He famously said that *"customers don't know what they want until we've shown them"*. He had an amazing foresight to develop products that consumers crave after, but more especially the boldness and courage to bring them into reality.

His followers were sold on his charisma – but he allowed others to play the game and help share his ideas. He is known to have taken his top 100 people away, bring in a whiteboard and ask them for their ideas for the top 10 "next things". Once the list was ready he would slash the bottom 7 and announce "we can only do 3". Focus was his calling card. He said *"deciding what not to do is as important as deciding what to do"*.

However, whilst his success often relied on him being an innovator – he was viewed by some as not always being a great leader. Jobs may have been as Walter Isaacson his biographer says, "the greatest business executive of our era", but he was a mercurial, demanding and sometimes a tyrannical one. Isaacson argues Jobs was not a saint and he did have rough edges: *"His petulance and impatience were part and parcel of his perfectionism"*.

Further: *"He acted as if the normal rules didn't apply to him, and the passion, intensity and extreme emotionalism he brought to everyday life were things he also poured into the products he made"*. It was his ability to innovate and anticipate that probably balanced his gruff persona.

Was he an honest leader?

This is a tough question to answer. He was not only successful – he became a global business icon. But Jobs' leadership style was complex. When he desired he was intensely focused; he was confident to follow his ideas and visions and held sway over legions through a deeply enduring character.

But in the age of transparent leadership, he was seen to be impatient, stubborn and hypercritical. He often dismissed potentially great ideas as a *"piece of crap"*, simply because they did not quite gel with his idea of the vision. Fortune magazine said of Jobs, his *"inhuman drive for perfection can burn out even the most motivated worker"*. Leander Kahney, one of Jobs biography authors, claimed his verbal assaults on staff, replete with anger and foul language, were terrifying. Fortune magazine dubbed Jobs as *"one of Silicon Valley's leading egomaniacs"*.

Equally, for such a leader who was arguably in touch with every aspect of his business, the installation of video cameras over engineers work stations, the claimed lack of knowledge over the poor working conditions in China (14 Foxconn employees working on Apple products committed suicide) and an internal communication policy that operated on a "need to know" basis does not inspire some to view Jobs as honest.

Nevertheless, many employees who left Apple often have a grudging respect and some even returned for more of his leadership abuse. For many, his style was not honest from an open leadership perspective – but it was his version of honesty, which for many hundreds of employees and millions of customers worked.

Followship is about following leaders. But what about followers who do not follow? Why may that be? If this can be identified, then surely we could better understand the whole concept of followship and leadership as one entity. The reasons we may choose not to follow will always be personal, but here are some ideas:

Refusal: Of course, some of us may not always accept the invitation. There may be many reasons not to follow but they are likely to be things such as not buying into the vision or we do not intellectually agree with the direction. Or maybe we simply do not care to work for the leader concerned. Overcoming refusal is critical; otherwise there is no one to lead.

Desertion: This is followship gone wrong. For whatever reason the follower has left and no longer wants to follow. In the army, deserters are put on trial and imprisoned. In business they are replaced and given a terrible reference. In our private life they are remembered, sometimes forgotten but never forgiven. Many of us desert through disappointment, where we feel an initial promise is not fulfilled. This can come from poor leadership. It can also come from unrealistic expectations where the follower is expecting a saviour rather than a leader.

As with leadership, the concept of followship has also been the subject of focus for some writers. After all, it is mostly the followers and not the leaders who actually get the work done. The followers amongst us tend to be closer to the pulse of the organisation or the centre of activity, such as the front line facing a customer. This is not always true for a leader. The drivers of followship may therefore be more important than those of the leader. In the book "The Power of Followship" by Robert Kelley, five different follower styles were identified, which are based on the followers willingness to think and act.

Alienated followers: Alienated followers are those who believe that we are free thinkers and independent individuals who do not willingly commit to any leader. We are capable but critical and without supervision will rarely produce results. We will follow or desert when it suits us and not the leader.

Passive followers (sheep): Passive followers are those of us who do as we are told. We do not think critically and we are not particularly active participants. We often seem to have time on our hands and are happy to wait for instructions.

Conformist followers (yes people): Those of you who are conformists are more participative than passive followers and generally allow your leader to do the thinking for you. You get on with the process and present little challenge, even if you know it is the wrong thing to do.

Pragmatic followers: Pragmatic followers like to weigh things up at the time and judge the expected outcome and its impact on their survival or career enhancement and balance this against the required effort. If this is you, it may mean that you are a drag on your leaders aspirations if you believe they offer neither personal advantage nor disadvantage to follow.

Exemplary followers (stars): Exemplary followers are ideal in almost all ways, excelling at all tasks, engaging strongly with the group and providing intelligent yet sensitive support and challenge to the leader. However, they must have immense courage to speak up at times and great integrity to know right from wrong.

Barbara Kellerman, a lecturer at Harvard, has described a similar typology of followship based on the level of engagement. She argues that good followers will actively support effective and ethical leaders and respond appropriately to bad leaders. In contrast, bad followers are seen as making no contribution and supporting the wrong types of leader. In this respect she also groups followers into five types, but in doing so attempts to look beyond the business environment.

Isolates: If you are an isolate you do not care or respond well to being led, but tend to just knuckle down and get the job done. You will do what you must and keep your head down. Kellerman argues that a typical isolate is someone, for example, who is eligible to vote, but probably chooses not to exercise that right.

Bystanders: Bystanders are just that; standing to one side, watching almost as an observer and going along passively but offering little active support.

Participants: If you are a participant you care about the organisation and try to make an impact. If you agree with the leader you will support him, but if you disagree, you may oppose him.

Activists: Activists feel more strongly about their organisations and leaders and act accordingly. When supportive, they are eager, energetic and engaged. When they are not supportive they can however be disruptive and create challenges for the leader to control.

Diehards: Are you a diehard? If so you are passionate about an idea, a leader or both and will give all for them. When you consider something worthy, you are dedicated.

It is beyond the scope of the pages to argue for or against the validity of the models (or to introduce even more), but from a leaders perspective it may be interesting to consider the preferred leadership approach and identify the kind of followship that offers best fit. If you prefer to practice a coercive "do as I say and not as I do" approach, a team of activists and exemplary followers may not be ideal to your cause. Rather I'd be looking for a team of conformists.

Bearing all this in mind, I believe that in order to have an influence over followers, leaders must have some pretty great characteristics. Do we therefore find the roots of leadership honesty – and therefore commitment from their followers – buried in the characteristics of leaders? Is it important to understand how leaders lead and generate trust?

WHAT MAKES A GREAT LEADER?

There are literally thousands – no millions of ideas about leadership characteristics. If you do not believe me go ahead and Google "Leadership Characteristics" and I will bet the price of this book you get more than 5 million results. So let's make some things clear before I start – I did not read all of the articles! We are interested in honest leadership – it's why I spent months writing and you are spending hours reading. Therefore I follow with a succinct summary of only those characteristics that I believe are most important to our understanding of an honest leader.

By that I am referring to the leader as a representative of authenticity and truth, one who can encourage honest open dialogue rather than focus only on the tasks at hand to get things done. By deliberately focusing on these softer angles I am avoiding some of the transactional aspects. In doing this I am not saying they are not important – they are – but for our purposes "getting things done" is not the same as "doing the right things".

Within these millions of articles you will find that some researchers claim a superior leader possesses certain character traits or abilities; others say it's all about personality. Still others argue it's the leaders' behaviours and has nothing to do with traits, abilities or personality. So what are we supposed to be believe?

According to dictionary.com, a character is *"the aggregate of features and traits that form the individual nature of some person or thing"*. Typically, characters will develop over time and are a result of the various inputs and experiences we receive. Our observable behaviour is an indication of our character. This behaviour can be strong or weak, good or bad. A person with strong character is likely to be more observable as they have a tendency to demonstrate drive, energy, determination, passion, self-discipline, willpower, an extroverted demeanour and courage. They may more easily attract followers. On the other hand, a person with a weak character tends to be shy, quiet, unassuming, hesitant and easily persuaded.

Having the traits that are associated to a good character does not mean that you are a good person, or even a good leader. Hitler demonstrated he was a strong person, a master orator and a smart leader – he was inspiring, motivating, passionate and determined. He was a man of vision who could sell his ideas and unite a nation. But morally – well we all know where he stood on that. And that is the missing ingredient that would otherwise make him great.

Adolf Hitler – An honest leader?

Who was he?

Hitler was Head of the NSDP (National Socialist German Workers Party) from 1921, founder of Nazism and the Chancellor and Führer of Germany 1933 – 1945. He was also author of "Mein Kampf" (My struggle), which rather famously outlined his views on an idealistic German society based on what many today would brand as blatant racism and fascism.

What did he do?

I presume I do not have to write too much here, suffice to say for those who never paid attention in history class you should be aware that the invasion of Poland in 1939 – in the interests of creating "Lebensraum" (living space) – probably kicked off World War II. It is estimated the war finally cost around 60 million lives. The radicalism behind his supremacist and racist policies led to his approval of the holocaust and the systematic murder of so called racial inferiors; around 11 million are believed to have lost their lives.

What's interesting about him?

We cannot eulogize about the things that Hitler did, but we can be fascinated about the way he did them. Ian Kershaw, author of the Hitler biography, describes Hitler as a *"bizarre, mediocre and wholly unpleasant"* person. But at the same time, Kershaw argues he held an almost inexplicable magnetism with the German people. He was an oratory master and milked the propaganda machine to its maximum, combining the historic values of "true heroic leadership" with a demonstrable and almost fanatical passion for his ideals.

This made him more than just inspiring – he became a symbol of the "solution to the struggle" and represented an ideology that suited the economic needs of the time.

Was he an honest leader?

The obvious answer is no. Of course not. He was a tyrant and a bully. He followed the idea of the "Führerprinzip", which for all intents and purposes put Hitler above written law – it was not just a directive style – it was the birth of fascism. His government formed a triangle with him at the apex where he enjoyed absolute rule.

But from another perspective, his stance on the political and social challenges facing Germany in his day was clearly outlined in his book "Mein Kampf". This included his beliefs and ideological thoughts and served as his philosophical platform from which he launched his bid for leadership. Granted, his approaches do not resonate well with the modern ideas surrounding ethical and moral leadership, and thus in this respect he was not an honest leader – but he was open and in his mind, it was his truth.

Compared to modern thinking, his leadership behaviour and approach also raises eyebrows. For example, he would commonly issue conflicting verbal orders with overlapping responsibilities – the idea being that the stronger subordinate would be identified through natural selection and do the job. He fostered competition, infighting and mistrust within his direct reports, which further consolidated his power base.

In concluding, it is perhaps worth asking ourselves whether Hitler would be as "successful" today as he was 70 years ago. Perhaps in a Europe suffering from austerity and economic hardship he would gain some support, but today our understanding of "good leadership" is more developed. We insist that leaders must be responsible to society and we see evidence of this through fallen dictatorships and imprisonment of corrupt CEO's.

Authors and professors James Kouzes and Barry Posner, in their book "The truth about Leadership", described "ten truths" within which leadership characteristics, behaviours and capabilities are outlined. After years of research, they argue that one consistent quality that is desirable in a leader is "credibility". Their research concluded that four traits contributed to leadership credibility:

Honesty: Honest leaders not only tell the truth, they also live it using a set of ethics and clear standards. They are virtuous and noble people.

Forward-Looking: Good leaders have a vision and are able to connect this to the hopes and aspirations of their followers. They are curious and possess certain courage to sell the vision and create a common approach to success.

Inspiring: Inspiring leaders have a positive attitude and can transmit this passion to others.

Competent: Competent individuals have a proven track record for getting things done. They are consistent, reliable and stable. This generates confidence in a leader.

They argued that researchers usually evaluate leaders based on their perceived trustworthiness, expertise and dynamism. These qualities are similar to being honest, competent and inspiring. So it would appear that one of the overriding traits of a good leader is honesty with a supporting set of characteristics that encourage the ability to develop and sustain trust in an organisation and its leadership.

To ensure trust levels are maintained, leaders need to ooze transparency and integrate this into a consistent communication approach. Leaders have a responsibility to make sure a code of ethics exists and more importantly that they adhere to this specific code in all of their dealings with their followers, customers and other stakeholders.

In this respect, I argue that other characteristics of trustworthy leaders should include:

Integrity: This is the ability of a leader to adhere to moral and ethical principles and do the right things.

Responsibility: Leaders should be aware that they are responsible for their success and that of their followers, and that they are accountable for personal and team actions.

Reliability: Reliable leaders are those who follow up on promises, deliver on agreements and do what they say they will, when they say they will.

Fairness: Leaders should not show favouritism and should treat people with an even hand and without prejudice.

Caring: Leaders should be able to encourage an open candid conversation about feelings and concerns and provide an open door.

If honest and trustworthy leaders reflect all or many of these characteristics, how then may we expect them to behave? Presumably they will be predictable and consistent, inspiring confidence and stability from followers. They will be excellent communicators, remaining clear, concise and structured. They will likely demonstrate empathy and listen with understanding and show respect.

They may well be prepared to take risks in their demonstration of courage. They will be bold and daring in their actions and proposals. But at the same time they will be humble and admit mistakes and should not enjoy finger pointing or apportioning blame. They will demonstrate humility and will not brag or use names and be able to be forthright or candid enough to express concern without exposing any vulnerability.

If we absorb all of these many traits and behaviours, it would seem that an honest leader must be lots of things. All the words, descriptions and behaviours seem incredibly inspirational and almost "perfect" don't they? But let's also be realistic – expecting a leader "to be" all of these things all of the time might be a lot to ask. Can we presume therefore that any leader that displays all or many of these items must be consistently good? Well, no. Not necessarily.

Returning to Joanne Ciulla she argued that consistency is the toughest challenge for leaders to master. In her paper "what is good leadership" she states *"leaders have to be more meticulous than ordinary people. First, because a leaders moral inconsistencies are public and more noticeable… and second, because a leaders credibility rests on some level of consistency"*.

A leaders' actions must align to values – otherwise they lose the trust they need to be effective. She uses the US foreign policy as a fine example where US leaders often advocate certain values and principles but do not apply them evenly around the world. Why, for example, was Iraq invaded yet the Syrian population deserted? We can only proffer assumptions, but I'll bet oil and regional interest play a large part. Leaders who only talk about moral values are hypocrites – they have to follow them through consistently.

I think therefore, that theory and practice are two different things. Fenwick English, in the "Art of Educational Leadership" wrote: *"The first act of leadership is coming to grips with yourself, who you are, where you are, and what is of value to you, and shaping yourself by acts of conscious will into what you want to become"*.

With this in mind, the approach that leaders use to lead – the manifestation of their individual behaviours into every day interactions to influence and persuade others, therefore becomes worthy of consideration.

How do leaders actually lead?

The way leaders bring their characteristics to bear is reflected by the manner and approach – or their style – they use to provide direction, implement plans and motivate people. In effect it is the pattern of behaviour a leader uses to influence people. The US Army Leadership manual offers its version of leadership influence *"Influencing is getting people... to do what is necessary. Influencing entails more than simply passing along orders. Personal examples are as important as spoken words. Leaders set that example, good or bad, with every action taken and word spoken, on or off duty. Through words and personal example, leaders communicate purpose, direction and motivation".*

Moving on from the military perspective, it is argued by many authors that the breadth of the different styles used will determine the effectiveness of a leader, although it should be noted that there is no right or wrong style. The leaders amongst us will gravitate towards a style that feels natural, this being influenced by our emotions, opinions, experiences, politics, competencies and attitudes. This style may also be strongly influenced and even determined by the personality, attitudes or capabilities of our followers.

Daniel Goleman and his co-authors Richard Boyatzis and Annie McKee argue in their book "Primal Leadership" that we often sit back and attempt to explain the effectiveness of our leaders through their ability to create visions, powerful ideas or be wonderfully strategic. But they argue the reality is that great leadership works through emotions. It does not matter what our leaders are trying to do, their ultimate success depends on their ability to drive our emotions. The way leaders do this – or the style and approach they use, is critical.

One of the core arguments is that emotions are essentially contagious, and thus a leader's attitude and energy can "infect" a workplace either for better or for worse. Goleman stated: *"The importance of a leaders mood and the attendant behaviours is surprising. That powerful pair set off a chain reaction. The leaders' mood and behaviours drive the moods and behaviours of everyone else. A cranky and ruthless boss creates a toxic organisation filled with negative underachievers who ignore opportunities; an inspirational, inclusive leader spawns acolytes for whom any challenge is surmountable".*

> *"A cranky and ruthless boss creates a toxic organisation filled with underachievers"*

Therefore he and his colleagues argue that leaders must demonstrate high self-awareness, which includes the ability to perceive and moderate the effect they are having on us.

Goleman called this ability "resonance", and argued leaders who resonate are able to speak authentically about their own values and beliefs and align [resonate] with the emotions of those who surround them. Resonance comes naturally to those with a high degree of Emotional Intelligence.

Creation of resonance can according to Goleman and his colleagues be done in 6 key ways. These "ways" are often referred to as leadership styles, and commonly used by global organisations and consultancies teaching leadership. I have adapted and collated the various interpretations as follows.

Visionary: This style is most appropriate when an organisation needs a new direction. Visionary styles move people towards a new set of shared dreams. *"Visionary leaders articulate where a group is going, but not how it will get there – setting people free to innovate, experiment, take calculated risks"* writes Goleman and his co-authors.

Coaching: This one-on-one style focuses on developing individuals and letting them find their own solutions, whilst showing them how to improve their performance and helping them to connect their goals to the goals of the organisation. Coaching works best *"with employees who show initiative and want more professional development".*

Affiliative: This style emphasises the importance of teamwork and creates harmony in a group by connecting people to each other. It boosts team morale and helps solve conflicts. Goleman argues this approach is particularly valuable *"when trying to heighten team harmony, increase morale, improve communication or repair broken trust in an organisation".*

Democratic/Participative: Leaders who use this approach draw on their followers' knowledge and skills and create a group commitment to the resulting goals. They value the teams input and get commitment through participation. However, this approach is not ideal in times of crisis, when urgent events demand quick decisions.

Pacesetting: When a leader is pacesetting, they set high standards for performance, often displaying a "do it my way" approach. Leaders are often *"obsessive about doing things better and faster and ask the same of everyone."* It is low on empathy but is useful when meeting challenging or exciting goals. However, this style can undercut morale and engender the feeling of failure amongst direct reports.

Commanding/Directive: Probably the most often used, but nevertheless the least effective, it is the typical "do it because I say so" approach. It rarely involves praise and frequently employs criticism; it undercuts morale and job satisfaction, but is useful in a crisis when an urgent turnaround is needed. Military leaders are often directive.

When thinking about different leadership styles, it is important to understand that they cannot be "used" in the same way as when buying a new outfit. We cannot try them on for size to see which fits best. Rather, leaders should be able to demonstrate a skill set that allows them to "flex" their style according to the situation they are in and the people they are with. Critical is that the leader is able to recognise these variables and diagnose their ability to make use of the full array of styles.

Barack Obama – An honest leader?

Who is he?

Obama is the 44th President of the United States (the first of African-American descent), a democrat, an ex-Illinois state Senator and a graduate of the Harvard Law School

What does he do?

Clearly as US President there are a whole host of activities that I could add to this paragraph. However, it probably makes more sense to focus on some of the more significant events that have marked his presidency to date, such as the official withdrawal of US troops from combat in Iraq or the introduction of a host of economic packages that his supporters argue saved the US from economic ruin during the crisis of 2008 – 2010.

He also was decisive in the rescue of US stalwarts GM and Chrysler and thousands of associated jobs; a new healthcare act that provides universal health care for the first time in the US and stood behind the activity that resulted in the death of Bin Laden, one of the worlds most wanted terrorists. Not a bad count over his first few years in office.

What's interesting about him?

Expressing puzzlement over questions about whether he is *"black enough"*, Obama told an August 2007 meeting of the National Association of Black Journalists that *"we're still locked in this notion that if you appeal to white folks then there must be something wrong"*.

Obamas background as a highly educated, Ivy League African-American is quite different to other coloured leaders who have risen out of the civil rights activities of the 1960's. He is of mixed race, young, smart and articulate and does not need to yell for "reparations" into the nearest microphone.

Obama is seen as an accomplished orator and a leader with charm and charisma. Oddly enough, however, he does not use his position or this skill to influence others in politics, but rather on doing the things he believes to be right. Obama spent many years in community groups, universities and legislatures and has developed a non-hierarchical style. He therefore sees issues from several points at once, meaning he can negotiate and balance different points of view.

But this is also his curse – many, often left wing republicans, argue that he cannot master the minefield of Congress and is too weak, seeking to avoid confrontation. Jesse Jackson is known to have said "*I think sometimes he wants to heal the wound by taking the glass out*". David Brooks, a columnist in the New York Times recently wrote: "*The job has overwhelmed the man. He's not an alien, he's not a radical. He's just not the person the country needs. He's not tough enough, he's not imaginative enough, and he's not determined enough*".

Is he an honest leader?

When President Obama was elected, he seemed like a different kind of leader. Not just the first coloured man in the White House but a new sort of American president: thoughtful, reflective, honest and determined to represent all of his country.

He started well, from his work on the economic bailouts of 2009, through to his focus on international wars, terrorism and the reform of healthcare. He has demonstrated a skill as referee who reminds us of our mistakes and offers choice and solutions beyond trying to simply polarise opinion. I get the feeling he genuinely cares and wants to make a difference.

But over the years he has been heavily criticised for losing his way and his clarity. He is accused of taking too long to make decisions and seeking too much. Republicans are of course the harshest critics. Ed Rogers, a veteran of the Bush and Reagan White House, told a BBC reporter "*I think Obama is not a very effective leader. I think he is a thinker and a ditherer to a fault. I think his leadership style does not lend itself to crisp decision making. I get the impression he anguishes before a decision, and even worse for a president, he anguishes after a decision*".

Others argue that Obama is not dithering, rather it is his desire to make the right pragmatic decision, and in doing that, be secure in the knowledge that he is as informed as he can be. For instance according to a BBC article, Paul Volker, the Chairman of the Federal Reserve was showing financial data to Obama, who insisted in diving deep into detail. Volker is said to have remarked "*I can't believe the president was interested in that*". He makes the point that Obama probably stopped the economy going "*off the edge of a cliff*".

It would appear that the jury is still out on Obama. He has been re-elected to a second term, but will he succeed? Ron Suskind, a US author critically covering Obamas handling of the economic crisis stated, *"I think he is a leader with extraordinary capacities. He is brilliant. The question that emerges is, 'is his brilliance the kind that makes for great presidents?' The kind that creates a distillate of decisiveness? That remains to be seen... this is his moment."*

This is true for every leader. It is not just about getting the leadership at the top to set the gold standard for other leaders [in an organisation, sports team or a political movement]. The style and approach of every leader must be such that inspiration permeates all levels. All leaders must be capable of building trust and resonating with all of us; all leaders must be able to understand that their emotions are contributing to the organisational environment within which we operate.

But it is also important to understand that leaders are not in place to make friends. Deborah Norville, US TV anchor said, *"If you want to be liked, get a dog. The people you work with are not your friends"*. Top dogs have a job to do. They must motivate, sell visions, inspire and lead change amongst many other things. Leaders must try to balance their styles against their objectives and the personalities they must work with. Being everyone's friend will not achieve results in the long run.

In this respect great leaders must understand that positive emotions are the flag bearer for a positive leadership style and these positive emotions will enhance good quality relationships with our leaders that are built on trust and respect.

You might have noticed that this idea of trust, ethical thinking, moral decision taking and team respect has been a consistent tone throughout this second part of our journey as it is my belief that this is fundamental to achieving honest leadership. Joanne Ciulla noted: *"In leadership we see morality magnified"*. I allow myself to use this as confirmation from another expert that an effective leader is not only productive, but is especially honest.

One of the more recent trends to have been much discussed is that of ethics. Much like "quality", "customer" and "loyalty" in the closing years of the last century, "ethics" and "integrity" have become the newer buzzwords when associated to leadership and organisational success in the intervening years. Gael O'Brien, a columnist for Business Ethics magazine stated *"Ethical leadership is one of the ways of keeping problems as problems before they become catastrophes"*.

ETHICAL LEADERSHIP – JUST A BUZZWORD?

The importance of ethics should not be underestimated. Most corporations and especially political leaders have a public image. This can impact our decisions in terms of what to buy, who to vote for, how and where to invest, what we should be like and so on.

Major scandals such as those from Enron, WorldCom and Tyco have raised concerns about ethics in business. Similarly the downfall of sports heroes such as Lance Armstrong following his admission to doping and the apparent never ending "Watergates" and news of affairs that surround politicians have brought ethics to the forefront of leadership thinking.

Indeed, today I have a feeling that we tend to write more about the morality and honesty of leaders than we do about their characteristics or capability to lead. And now ethics and by implication the ethical actions of all leaders are under the microscope. We judge our business, sports, religious or political leaders and expect them to be more accountable for their actions than ever before. During his election campaign in 1992 Bill Clinton blasted the behaviour of the incumbent Bush administration and pledged to conduct *"the most ethical administration in the history of the country"*. A few years later, when referring to his affair with Whitehouse intern Monica Lewinsky he stated in his speech to the Grand Jury *"I was wrong. It constituted a critical lapse in judgment and personal failure on my part"*. Well, at least that eventually cost him the trust of a nation.

Before we consider what ethical leadership is, we should understand what ethics actually are. What do we mean when we use the term "ethical"? The concept of "ethics" seems to have a fairly large reach. Today "ethics" has been associated with a variety of "do good" terms such as corporate social responsibility, fair trade, sustainability, ethical leadership, fair play, social enterprise, non-profit, well-being at work etc.

As a consequence there seems to be no universally applied set of rules, controls or expectations when one refers to ethics in modern society.

A simple definition of the word ethics would be "fair". The Oxford dictionary states that ethics are *"moral principles that govern a person's behaviour"*. And in turn it defines morality as *"principles concerning the distinction between right and wrong or good and bad behaviour"*.

In the context of our "honest leader", I think that an ethical leader is not just focussed on achieving results, but in ensuring that those results are achieved in the right way. Ethical leaders respect the rights and dignity of others and use their integrity based on their personal beliefs and values to stimulate trustworthiness to a very high level – these are critical components to leading ethically. Ethical leaders tend to be highly self-aware and people orientated and far less self-serving.

> *"Ethical leaders respect the rights and dignity of others"*

Many authors argue that ethical leaders are more effective. This probably seems like a no brainer but it may not always be true; sometimes thinking ethically can be costly. The President of Toyota for example made the decision to recall around seven million vehicles between 2010 – 2011 for possible unexpected acceleration problems, caused in part by incorrectly placed floor mats and in part by sticking accelerator pedals. His decision was driven by ethical and safety issues and concern for customer well-being.

However, due to a delay in receiving parts combined with massive media exposure due to the size of the recall, many owners jumped onto a psychological bandwagon and claimed wrongful deaths and accidents as a result of the car problems. All claims were subsequently proven to be a mix of driver error or hoaxes, but not without first costing Toyota millions of dollars in legal defence and lost sales and prompted a share price fall of 16%, from a high of around $90.

Consider also the case of the Swiss charity Christian Solidarity International who wanted to free upwards of 200,000 children in Sudan from slavery. They paid between $35 and $75 per head for their freedom, but in doing this inadvertently created a market for slavery and therefore exacerbated the problem, driving the demand and prices for slaves higher. Joanne Ciulla argues that difficult moral decisions are risky as leaders often lack control over the variables to determine the outcome – but leaders are worthy of forgiveness when they act with care for the right moral reasons.

We should be aware that having and following personal ethics is not the same as having certain ingrained characteristics. We are who we are, which means that we cannot simply change the traits we possess. But ethics are more dynamic and they need self-knowledge and self-control. Ethics are only ethical if we practice them – otherwise they remain ideals. I may value ethical thinking – but it does not mean I always tell the truth. Ethics are good habits that we learn from society, parents, teachers and our leaders and in some cases are even formally publicised for us to follow.

For example, many organisations today issue ethical codes of conduct. These are a statement of a company's responsibilities to its employees, customers, suppliers and the community and help guide our leaders in their pursuit of morality and honesty. However, the codes do not often spell out specific do's and don'ts or suggest proper behaviour, but rather give broad guidelines within which we are expected to find our own ethical balance, regardless of whether we are employees or leaders.

Apple & Microsoft for example, issue short but succinct codes of conduct that cover the expectations of employees in dealing with issues such as customer & supplier relationships, financial matters, conflict of interest, insider trading, gifts, intellectual property and so on. The introduction to the Code from Microsoft touches on many of the aspects we have raised about leadership and their activities:

*"Microsoft aspires to be a great company, and our success depends on you. It depends on people who innovate and are committed to growing our business responsibly. People who dedicate themselves to really satisfying customers, helping partners and improving the communities in which we do business. People, who are accountable for achieving big, bold goals with unwavering integrity. **People who are leaders, who appreciate that to be truly great, we must continually strive to do better ourselves and help others improve.***

We must expect the best from ourselves, because who we are as a company and as individuals is as important as our ability to deliver the best products and services. How we manage our business internally – and how we think about and work with customers, partners, governments, vendors and communities – impacts our productivity and success. **It's not enough to just do the right things; we have to do them in the right way"**

The common thread found in the communication from many global organisations demonstrates a continued focus on leadership ethics. From **BMW: "Sustainable action starts with a mind-set.** The entire Board of Management of the BMW Group is represented on our Sustainability Board. Every day, over 96,000 employees worldwide are working to achieve further progress across the entire value chain. This is true for our business and also for our partnerships and our relationships with all stakeholders".

Introducing their Code of Conduct Honeywell state: **Honeywell places a high value on the integrity of the company and our directors, officers, employees and representatives. Our reputation and our brand name mean a lot to us. From the shop floor to the boardroom,** all Honeywell employees and representatives are expected to comply with all laws and regulations in the countries where we do business."

Johnson & Johnson, when referring to their code of conduct state "the values that guide our decision making are spelled out in our Credo. Our Credo challenges us to put the needs and well-being of the people we serve first". Our Credo "sets forth our core values and business philosophy. **It is the moral compass that guides our responsibilities**…. The principles in our Credo reflect the character, ethics and values that define us as a Company and lay the foundation for the **expectations we have for our directors, management and employees in operating a responsible company**…. The values embodied in our Credo **guide the actions of the people** of the Johnson & Johnson Family of Companies **at all levels, including directors and officers. The ethical character and integrity of Johnson & Johnson Directors and Executive Officers are considered one of the most important safeguards of corporate governance".**

And finally BP, perhaps because of recent oil spill disasters focus on honesty and ethical business throughout its organisation: "What we do is rarely easy. Achieving the best outcomes often requires the courage to face difficulty, **to speak up and stand by what we believe. We always strive to do the right thing. We explore new ways of** *thinking and are unafraid to ask for help. We are honest with ourselves, and actively seek feedback from others.* *We aim for an enduring legacy, despite the short term priorities of our world".*

I have highlighted those aspects of the ethical codes I believe of specific relevance to our topic. Of course, from our perspective when considering ethical leadership, any code of ethical conduct is meaningless if we as employees, and in particular our leaders, do not adhere to it when making decisions. If our leaders continue to push us for bottom line results, the chances are that they are building a culture that implicitly supports us to engage in unethical behaviour to get ahead.

As Ciulla noted, *"ethical leadership entails the ability of leaders to sustain fundamental notions of morality such as care and respect for persons, justice and honesty, in changing organisational, social and global contexts".* We are only just beginning to scratch the surface of understanding ethics and leadership, but what is already clear is that our search for honest leadership is valid and right up to the minute.

But in the days when companies measure the return on everything and cut things that can't be measured, how do we even justify being ethical and honest? What's the impact on the bottom line? In short, does being honest pay off? Is it worthwhile to be a top dog? And if so, how does one go about being more honest? These aspects and more we will discuss in Part III.

QUESTIONS FOR SELF-REFLECTION

So we have reached the end of Part II and it's time to excite your grey cells and ask yourself about your leadership characteristics, attitude, style and behaviours. Are you an honest leader and if not why not?

- Are you a leader or a manager? Which should you be?
- Can you describe your leadership style? Would your followers agree with you?
- Do your followers respect you for your position or the things you have done for them?
- Are you trustworthy? Why?
- Are you inspirational? Why?
- Can you articulate your personal or organisational ethical code of conduct? Do you follow it?
- Why do you follow other leaders? Do you want to or must you?

PART III
REALISING THE BENEFITS

"If you do not look at things on a large scale, it will be difficult to master strategy."
– Miyamoto Mursashi

"Leaders don't wait. They shape their own frontiers. The bigger the challenge, the greater the opportunity."
– Unknown

"Earn your success based on service to others; not at the expense of others."
– H. Jackson-Brown Jr.

Are you an honest leader? Do you want to be? And if you decide that you do, then maybe you have some work to do.

But becoming more honest is not just a case of "not lying". It is easier said than done. Just not lying is for many the moral equivalent of "just not smoking" or "just not drinking". But unlike these examples we have no "liars patch" or "liars anonymous" we can turn to, to help us through our withdrawal symptoms and onto a journey of discovery – rather honesty starts with ourselves, we cannot pass the buck.

Before we tackle the above however we must first figure out if all the effort is worth it. Today we have to demonstrate to different stakeholders that our actions and decisions generate a payback – be that quantitative or qualitative. We must analyse whether honesty can pay off and really contribute to the bottom line, or whether it is an ideal best avoided.

Does honesty pay?

Well that's the $1,000,000 question isn't it? All too often business will not get passionate about touchy feely and emotional things unless there is a direct measureable benefit. More often than not our leaders only approve capital investment and embark on new strategies when there is a robust business case. An increase in sales or a boost in revenues, in margins or in efficiencies must be demonstrable. Better still, combine this with decreases in costs and inefficiencies and you just may get your ideas through. "Being honest" and "doing the right thing", although morally correct, does not always cut it at board level when it comes to justifying a business case.

How many times have you heard this? In today's world pretty often, I assume. For those of you involved in touchy feely people development activities you may agree that it is no longer a rarity to have your annual departmental budgets spliced, downsized, repackaged or just plain deleted because the benefit of your activities cannot always be directly measured.

Or at the very least you are asked to measure the financial effectiveness of things that just can't be reliably measured. You have to demonstrate added value. Consider the request for example to measure the *direct* financial impact of a development programme that focuses on increasing a leader's ability to enhance morale, inspiration and motivation in their teams. Or to measure the increase in unit sales that we get from an employee as a *direct* result of their attendance to a sales training.

Sure, we could use some indirect indicators. For leadership effectiveness we can use indicators such as talent retention, employee engagement, satisfaction ratings, employee turnover, organisational climate studies, leadership style measures and personality surveys; or in sales we could use data that measures conversion rates, lost bids, profitability and upsell success for example. But it is not an easy task, if nigh on impossible, to measure *direct* financial impact of soft skills initiatives in an organisation.

The challenge is that there are many other factors that can impact financial performance. It takes more than just a highly skilled sales guy or great motivational leaders to influence the financial data. And besides, what number – what reliable, proven, tested and consistent indicator – can we use to measure the financial result of for instance an employee being more or less motivated, or employee engagement following the introduction of a corporate social responsibility programme?

Therefore we often have to rely on "gut feel" that doing some of these things is simply the "right thing to do" and try to determine how much effort and financial commitment the powers that be are prepared to accept. Consequently the question becomes not only *"can I do moral things"* but also *"how right, moral or honest do I want to be*?" and how far can I go before hard financial returns are being questioned?

Of course, with these questions come the experts and professors who try to find answers for us. They build study after study and publish their results in acclaimed journals for us to read and perhaps even use, as we try to support our business cases and justify our decisions. And this is exactly the point we have reached on our journey – to try to understand if it is worthwhile being an honest leader, not only for yourself (which is more of a personal consideration) but also for your followers and if relevant for your organisations.

THE QUANTITATIVE VIEW

It presumably makes sense to start with measurable things as I am sure you will agree these are more attractive to our pragmatically minded decision makers and company leaders – especially profit. By this I refer to margins and other bottom line stuff that attracts shareholders, keeps the tills ringing and stock markets happy. We need to understand if "honesty" has a place in a profit-orientated organisation. In other words, does it even make (financial) sense?

And this is a tough one to answer. In the minds of many leaders in profit minded organisations, any activities that relate to "being honest" or "corporate morality" will often take the back burner. It is almost impossible to determine how "honesty" contributes to the bottom line.

The problem is that "honesty" is not on the balance sheet. It cannot be quantified and things that cannot be quantified are traditionally viewed with suspicion. Even if it was on the balance sheet, how could it be measured? It's just soft stuff right? Organisations do not need friends with whom they can dance around the balance sheet singing "cum by yah" – they need customers and they need investors to help them expand or stay competitive. And investors want returns – and by returns I do not mean good feelings, I mean profit. And for some investors honesty, morality and other soft stuff does not get a great deal of thinking time when compared to making money.

Therefore it narrows down to hard facts. Things like margins. Revenues. Shareholder value. Working capital. EBIT. Call it what you will, but any leader who cannot influence these things in an organisation is not going to get very far in today's world. These indicators of value and return theoretically demonstrate the stamina and success of our leaders and tend to be the drivers in today's global organisations. So much so that some see fit to manipulate these numbers and falsify reality for personal or organisational gain.

Financial numbers, it seems, must not only be positive but also on the rise – ideally time and again, year after year. And have you noticed how every year it's the same? Once one target is achieved, the next is laid in cement. Do we ever have enough? Therefore any strategic ideas or initiatives that require significant capital investment are likely to get studied with a careful, beady eye. All our activities must positively contribute towards the upward march of financial KPI.

It appears to be commonly accepted that the performance of top leaders in an organisation can heavily influence its profitability. And the value of an organisation (the price of its stock), and the success of our leaders are often based upon the decisions they take (what) rather than the "softer impacts" they make (how).

For instance, investment experts will rate stock as a "buy" or a "sell", finance institutions may extend or withdraw credit lines and so on, based often on *what* leaders do and achieve – but not often on *how* they do it. If it appears that these decisions will have a positive (or negative) impact on the future earnings of an organisation, the price of the stock will fluctuate up (or down) accordingly.

In the late 1990's Swissair, for example, embarked on an aggressive expansion plan – the so called "Hunter strategy" to challenge Europe's biggest and best and capture market share through acquisition. And so began a misguided leadership decision, in which Swissair purchased large, often overpriced equity stakes with non-profitable and largely "broken" European airlines such as Sabena, AOM, Portugalia (all of whom have never returned to the skies) to finally end up with around 10 airlines in its "Qualiflyer" alliance network.

Initially, this strategy of buying equity stakes seemed successful – despite net losses in 1995 & 1996, by 1997 it appeared to have turned the corner, and net cash from operations more than doubled from CHF969 million in 1997 to CHF2.1 billion in 1999. And although its net margin at 3% was still below the industry average, the share price according to the Bloomberg database raised from CHF226 at the beginning of 1997 to CHF509 barely 16 months later – a healthy 125% return in a remarkably short period of time.

Investors were convinced its strategy was the right approach and, despite a gradual decline, kept the share price well above the 1997 levels until 2001. But closer analysis of the investments the Management Board had made illustrated that whilst the Groups operations were profitable, the investment strategies were haemorrhaging cash to the tune of more than CHF3 billion in 2000. It was becoming clear that the "what" the leaders were doing – building market share – was not cleverly aligned to the "how" the leaders were doing it.

Therefore the Group did not have sufficient resource to recover from external shocks such as the US World Trade Centre attacks in 2001. By 2002, it was suffering from billions of Swiss francs in losses and had its equity tied up in non-profitable alliance partners which were facing re-structuring challenges. Swissair was in a corner. Combined with a dried up credit line, Swissair was forced to ground its fleet with the loss of thousands of jobs, personal and corporate investments, its reputation in tatters and the criticism and shame of a nation on its shoulders. In 2007 the management board was charged with mismanagement but ultimately cleared of wrongdoing.

A CEO is expected to spin a positive outlook on all corporate activities, regardless of how dire the situation may look. And sometimes the decisions they need to take may be at the expense of sound business strategy, honesty or moral thinking.

The drive for enhanced profitability drove Swiss bank UBS to announce 10,000 job losses in October 2012. On the same day, the share price rose 13%. The President of UBS seemed exceptionally calm in an interview with a Swiss online newspaper at the time. He remarked that his investment bankers should be used to this, as much like their job, it is not about respect but only about *"risk management"* – the implication being that they are now the risk.

But where is the morality in that kind of comment? What about the people? Whilst the value of the company is increased by hundreds of million Swiss francs, it appeared that any moral obligation to the people who helped get it there in the first instance was irrelevant. It was arguably not an honest or moral decision, but rather one driven by the need for (more) profit and ultimately the expectations of investors. Not without reason is UBS sometimes referred to as the *"United Bandits of Switzerland".*

And as we all know with share prices, they can move up as well as down. And there is evidence to suggest that share prices do dip if companies or leaders are seen to be "too honest" or show "too much integrity".

Toyota – An honest organisation?

Who are they?

Toyota Motor Corporation is the world's 11th largest company and vying for top spot with General Motors as the world's largest automobile manufacturer by production and sales. Give or take a few hundred thousand units, it shifts around 8 million cars annually.

Despite being headquartered in Japan, its global operations are considerable, building cars and dominating sales charts on every continent globally from the USA to Africa. It is easier to explain where they do not build cars rather than where they do.

Toyota products are as ubiquitous as washing machines (and about as interesting) with over 200 million cars being built since its inception in 1933. It owns a number of different brands including Lexus and Scion, has stakes in Daihatsu, Isuzu and Fuji heavy Industries, which is related to Subaru.

Are they successful?

The economic downturn and natural disasters in Japan and Thailand hit Toyota hard, but nevertheless it's a company that appears unstoppable. It appears often in the lists of the world's largest, wealthiest and most admired companies (published by the likes of CNN, Financial Times and Fortune) and reasonably consistently reports sales revenues around $210 billion. Before the crisis in 2009, it was rumoured to have had as much as $90 billion in cash in the bank. At that time it would have been sufficient to have purchased 100% of GM.

What makes them remarkable?

The Toyota Way. This is the company's management philosophy that sets Toyota apart from many of its competitors. It has consistently evolved its ideals since the early days and today, under the headings of Respect for People and Continuous Improvement, summarises its values around five main principles – Challenge (vision), Kaizen (improvement), Genchi Genbutsu (go to the source), Respect (mutual trust) and Teamwork.

With this in mind Toyota has carved itself a reputation as being something of a pioneer in the industry. For instance. it was instrumental in changing the face of motor vehicle production at a global level with its "Just in Time" production approach and other lean production methods.

Similarly, the philosophy of "Kaizen" was brought to public life when Toyota released the world's first hybrid production vehicle, the Prius, in 1997. Whilst many of its competitors were still playing in the laboratory, the Prius came to market with an innovative petrol electric hybrid motor that achieved near diesel matching levels of fuel efficiency and record breaking low levels of CO_2 emissions.

Despite a slow take up, three vehicle generations later and with use of the same technology in other Toyota & Lexus products, the company is today the words largest producer of hybrid motor vehicles, offering a broad selection of more than 15 models from luxury through to small city cars. Today it shifts around 500,000 units annually and has sold approximately four million hybrids since the introduction of the first Prius. It dominates this market.

This environmental orientated thinking has been a common theme at Toyota for years. Already by 2005, Toyota had released its fourth environmental action plan (they are now on their fifth) whilst others were releasing their first. These plans outline in broad terms its CSR and sustainability strategy, covering aspects such as automobile recycling, environmental protection and establishing a low carbon society.

Toyota openly states *"we intend to contribute by taking the lead in the sustainable development of society and the earth, sharing and implementing our CSR policy globally with the aim of becoming an admired and trusted company in the various regions where we conduct business"*. And to ensure it achieves this, Toyota created a CSR committee to oversee and align all corporate actions, including the introduction of a set of strategic CSR key performance indicators in recent years. These include safety, the environment, society and culture, energy and personnel development.

Does this approach win recognition?

Similar to other organisations with wide, deep and consistent CSR approaches, Toyota has also been recognised by the Dow Jones Sustainability Index (DJSI), the FTSE4Good index, the Morningstar socially responsible investment (MS-SRI) list and is a member of the Global 100 most sustainable corporations in the World.

For instance in 2012, Craig Kipp the CEO of Boart Longyear, a maker of exploratory mining drills was sacked for being too honest. And this was only one month after reporting record half year profits and an 89% increase for the six months prior to that. In essence, Kipp had not too wisely explained why the share price, which had remained stubbornly low, was unlikely to increase, as he believed the market had peaked. This spooked investors and as a result share prices fell 36%. A spokesperson for the company, when announcing the immediate departure of Kipp, indicated that they hoped to appoint someone with more experience in "engaging the market".

We have a similar story with David Robb, the CEO of Iluka. In 2012 he predicted low future demand for mineral sands, the core operation of Iluka. This warning sparked a 24%, or $1.1 billion plunge in organisational value, leaving analysts no choice but to madly slash the year's profit expectations by more than 50% and that of 2013 by as much as 40%. It could be argued that investors at least knew where they stood – but Robb's honest approach also prompted much criticism, with some analysts arguing that the job of a CEO is to be more positive and supportive – an "all-in or all-out" approach is not one that investors like to hear.

These examples demonstrate that the "*what*" of a leadership decision appears on many occasions to be more important than the "*how*". Investors are interested in getting a return. This is fair enough, why shouldn't they? But honesty or morality does not always seem to be a factor in this process. If these examples demonstrate anything, it is that being honest possibly does not pay, either for our leaders or for the organisations that allow them to thrive.

Regrettably we probably cannot change this thinking. It is the way it is. Or is it? I do not believe it has to be like this, do you? For example, Richard Branson, founder of the Virgin Group of companies once said: "*Above all you want to create something you are proud of… that is my philosophy of business. I can honestly say that I have never gone into business to make money. If this is the sole motive, then I believe you are better off doing nothing*". Today he runs an organisation of well over 200 separate entities and has a personal worth estimated to be in the region of $5 billion.

And Branson is not the only apparently moral yet financially successful leader. The table below summarises the financial performance of some large organisations and marries this to the "moral compass" that many of the organisational leaders have embedded into their thinking in the last 10 years – especially since "transparent" leadership and ethical business practices have become more acceptable.

Of course there are other organisations that have also performed well without encouraging their leaders to make ethics and morality a focal point of their approach, but the important message behind this summary is that morality and moral decision-making does not need to hinder profitability if an organisation provides the framework within which its leaders can morally operate.

Company	Moral compass	What's different about them	Sales Revenues 2010 & % change vs. FY 2000
ABB	Integrity, act responsibly	Integrity is at the core of all activities, embedded in corporate culture	$31.6 billion + 37.5%
Apple	Mobile freedom, simplicity, innovation	Revolutionised all aspects of data sharing and mobility, transformed several industries	$65 billion + 1300%
Disney	Make people happy	Introduced entertainment segmentation (theme parks, retail, film)	$38 billion + 52%
Intel	Connect & enrich the lives of every person on earth	Change the way every person can communicate, learn and live.	$43.6 billion + 32%
Johnson & Johnson	The Credo: Putting people first	Embedded the Credo philosophy for 50 years – reflected in all values and activities. It is the company DNA	$63 billion + 111%
Virgin	Business is about sustainable fun, not just profit	"Touchy feely" people orientated culture in all Virgin companies; challenging the norm.	$21 billion in 2011, estimated a 7 fold increase since 2000 (not publicly quoted)
Wal-Mart	Give customers a great deal	Introduced low price shopping mentality in small towns	$421 billion + 255%

Table inspired by Nikos Mourkogiannis in Strategy & Business magazine 2005

Nikos Mourkogiannis wrote in Strategy & Business magazine back in 2005: *"The most successful organisations over time are those, in which people act consistently and decisively, innovating and building high-quality relationships. The task of leadership is to stimulate these kinds of actions, reliably and continually. The executives who can do this are not magicians. Consciously or not, they have learned how to deploy a conceptual tool that allows them to inspire and lead an organisation toward enduring competitive advantage"*.

He argued that these leaders demonstrate moral purpose, which he defined as something that is held by us as being innately "right" and worthwhile. It is a demonstration of not just *"what"* but also *"how"* decisions are made. Leaders use both, the head and the heart, to guide us and point the direction for organisational strategy – and they are not "financially punished" for doing so.

In the same article he argued that "leader's morality" had different manifestations depending on the perspective – for example Sam Walton, founder of the world's largest grocery store Wal-Mart, was apparently tough and sometimes unforgiving. But he was driven by a higher reaching purpose that was *"giving customers a good deal"*. In his biography "Made in America", Walton said: *"There is only one boss. The customer. And he can fire everybody in the company from the chairman on down, simply by spending his money somewhere else"*.

And with this focus in mind, Walton spent his life putting customers first and ensuring his employees did the same. He named his employees "associates" and tapped into their good natured feelings to help other human beings. He believed that this would encourage employees to treat customers in a friendly and helpful way, which (combined with his fierce pursuit of low prices) established the kind of customer loyalty that has been the central competitive advantage of his company. Walton was successful because he walked the talk, communicating these beliefs at every turn.

Walton: *"The secret of successful retailing is to give your customers what they want. And really, if you think about it from the point of view of the customer, you want everything: a wide assortment of good quality merchandise; the lowest possible prices; guaranteed satisfaction with what you buy; friendly, knowledgeable service; convenient hours; free parking; a pleasant shopping experience."*

Of course, there are those who may not agree. Many argue that the smaller "mom & pop" businesses are pushed brutally to one side once Wal-Mart enters town. Indeed President Clinton's former secretary of Labour, Robert Reich, stated in an article in the New York Times in 2005 that Wal-Mart turns *"main streets into ghost towns by sucking business away from small retailers."*

Many believe that Wal-Mart is only run through self-interest to Wal-Mart rather than to other organisations and refer to the comments of Lee Scott, a former Wal-Mart CEO, who said *"we are not doing this for ethical reasons. We are doing it for good business"*. Maybe therefore they are right – for example, it is claimed that when Wal-Mart opened up in Iowa, 555 grocery stores, 298 hardware stores, 293 building suppliers, 161 variety shops, 158 women's stores, and 116 pharmacies all closed down.

But this cannot be statistically proven, as Andrea Dean and her co-author Russel Sobel from West Virginia University discovered in 2008. Their research concluded: *"After examining a plethora of different measures of small business activity and growth…. It can be firmly concluded that Wal-Mart has had no significant impact on the overall size and growth of U.S. small business activity"*. Whatever the truth, the numbers that underpin the business model speak for themselves, and today Wal-Mart is one of the biggest global supermarket chains.

In contrast, Apple finds its roots in innovation, in what Mourkogiannis termed *"Discovery for its own sake"*. This is driven by entrepreneurs such as Steve Jobs who actively encouraged an open environment of innovation and energetic creativity. Jobs, a modern day leadership icon, famously said *"customers don't know what they want until we've shown them"*. As we well know, his organisation went onto revolutionise the face of many industries from publishing through photography, music and mobile communications – and in doing so created the most valuable company in the world.

Intels leaders have taken a different approach, supporting the idea that moral & honest thinking is also a form of heroism. To install a vision that states *"create and extend computing technology to connect and enrich the lives of every person on earth"* requires a bold and visionary leader. I am not an Intel employee, but when I absorb this, consider its meaning, depth and breadth, I find it an exceptionally powerful statement. It makes you want to be a part of it.

Leaders at Intel refer to "inventing the future" and not waiting for it. It builds upon the ethos created by the company co-founder Robert Boyce, who said *"don't be encumbered by the past. Go off and do something wonderful"*.

Earlier Intel visions, such as *"to be the world's largest semi-conductor manufacturer"* and *"a billion connected computers around the world"* were equally heroic for their time and also considered to be unachievable. But Intel made it, spurred along by the likes of CEO Craig Barrett who said *"our commitment to doing the right things runs deep in our corporate culture"*.

Today, Intel is a vast global empire which can lay claim to its chips, motherboards, servers, ethernets and electronics being in nearly every PC, network and mobile computing device worldwide. Their culture is intended to energise employees to do the impossible, to dream and stretch themselves into new areas, currently considered as unachievable. They encourage passionate people to do passionate things – whatever that may be and wherever it may lead.

The leadership at Nestlé, one of the world's largest food and beverage organisations, focuses on "trust". Its corporate website: *"We believe that leadership is about behaviour, and we recognize that trust is earned over a long period of time by consistently delivering on our promises. Nestlé believes that it is only possible to create long-term sustainable value for our shareholders if our behaviour, strategies and operations also create value for the communities where we operate, for our business partners and of course, for our consumers"*. This philosophy has contributed to the success of Nestlé, that today reports annual revenues in the region of $85 billion and profit margins of 15%. Not bad for a company focusing on trust and honest leadership behaviour.

Nestlé – An honest organisation?

Who are they?

Nestlé is the world's leading nutrition, health and wellness company and has been named as one of Americas Most Admired Companies by Fortune for many years. It is probably best known for brands such as Perrier, Nesquik Chocolate Powder, Smarties, Kit Kat, Nespresso and Nescafé, although it is also a significant player in many other foods from dairy through to pet products.

Today the 150 year old Swiss based company employs around 330,000 people in over 150 countries and operates more than 450 factories in 83 countries.

Are they successful?

Yes. Despite a few ups and downs Nestlé consistently reports annual sales revenues in the range of CHF85 billion (read the same in US dollars), earnings per share around CHF3 and margins around 15%.

What makes them remarkable?

"Good food, good life" is the promise of Nestlé, and this is done via "*Creating Shared Value*" – a philosophical thinking which, in the same manner as at J&J, is consistently applied in many aspects of organisational culture, strategy and thinking. This quiet "get on with it", typical Swiss approach has helped Nestlé maintain its leadership position.

Nestlé claims that its Ten Corporate Business Principles, published as early as 1998, have their roots embedded within the company DNA. The Ten Principles cover six categories including consumers, human rights, people, suppliers, customers and the environment, each supported with its own explicit strategy. The principles represent the basic way in which Nestlé does business, which states that in order to create long term value for shareholders, they have to create value for society. This includes a focus on compliance, sustainability and acting in the best interest of our communities. Is this Nestlé operating "beyond corporate social responsibility"?

Its CEO, Paul Bulcke, stated in its annual report, "*We recognise that if we are going to build businesses that are successful today and sustainable tomorrow, we need to invest upstream and create value for our partners and contribute more broadly into the societies in which we operate"*. He followed this with approving a $25 million direct financial assistance to farmers in the dairy and coffee industries, educational assistance to children in Eastern Europe and sourcing healthy drinking water in rural Africa.

Of course many large corporates claim similar "do good" activities in their annual reports – but it is the sheer scale of the commitment that makes Nestlé stand out.

They have signed up as a founding member to all ten principles in the United Nations Global Compact and LEAD initiative; they voluntarily apply the World Health Organisation code, recognise the UN Framework on Business and Human Rights, are a part of several United Nations Global Compact (UNGC) working groups and are in regular contact with the International Labour Organisation (ILO) amongst many initiatives.

The Creating Shared Value Report is a nigh on 300 page volume covering the moral activities of Nestlé, including Nutrition, Water, People, Rural development and environmental sustainability. The work at Nestlé goes well beyond compliance. In its annual report, Nestlé states *"we will not sacrifice our principles and values for short term success. We believe that to build a profitable business we must create value for both, society and for our shareholders. This is what we mean by "creating shared value"*.

Does this approach win recognition?

Oh yes. Nestlé has been a high ranking winner within the Dow Jones Sustainability Index (DJSI) for several years in a row; it is a part of the FTSE4Good Index, The Stockholm Industry Water Award, has won the 2011 World Environment Centre Gold Medal for its on-going commitment to sustainable business and for the second year in a row joined the Carbon Disclosure Leadership Index for its proactive work to climate change.

Joe Hogan, the CEO of ABB, believes trust is found within integrity. He says *"we want to be the most successful and competitive company in our class, but we never want to compromise our integrity"*. Under his lead, ABB has launched an integrity based culture programme covering leadership & communications and has created a team of over 300 employees,each of whom help to ensure integrity is embedded into its activities. Hogan: *"Our integrity programme is being run relentlessly as a fully integrated business process, with zero tolerance toward illegal or unethical behaviour"*. These efforts have enabled ABB to post revenues in 2012 of $39 billion, and net margins of 10.3%. Integrity does not appear to be standing in the way of good financial return.

People form the moral compass and focus at Johnson & Johnson (J&J). The J&J "Credo" has been embedded in the organisational DNA since the 1940's, long before corporate morality and social responsibility was even considered important. According to J&J, its Credo challenges the organisation and its leaders to put the needs of the people it serves first: *"We believe our first responsibility is to the doctors, nurses and patients, to mothers and fathers and all others who use our products and services. In meeting their needs, everything we do must be of high quality… we are responsible to our employees, the men and women who work with us throughout the world. We must respect their dignity and recognise their merit…. We are responsible to the communities in which we live and work and to the world community as well"*.

This philosophy is as much present today as 50 years ago, with J&J proudly stating that it is *"caring for the world – one person at a time"*. This thinking and direction unites the thoughts and actions of the 129,000 employees across 60 countries.

Leaders such as Richard Branson demonstrate similar thinking, albeit with a touch more flair. He has said: *"Having a personality of caring about people is important. You can't be a good leader unless you generally like people. That is how you bring out the best in them"*. This moral philosophy is extended through the Virgin group of companies. Virgin has spent 40 years challenging the established blue chips in many of its target markets, with its unique twist on running a business. According to *Virgin* *"[we have] always stood for value for money, quality, innovation, fun and a sense of competitive challenge… we no longer have a list of brand values but a brand cube to which we have added the Wellbeing & Happiness of People and Sustainability of the Planet"*.

Richard Branson – An honest leader?

Who is he?

Sir Richard Branson is the man behind the Virgin brand, starting it in 1972 as Virgin records, and later expanding this to include an airline, Virgin Atlantic in the 1980's. Today the Virgin Group numbers more than 200 companies and Branson is said to be Britain's 4th richest man, with an estimated worth of more than $5 billion.

What does he do?

Branson is Virgin, Virgin is Branson. The two go hand in hand, feeding off of one another. He is a compass for the organisation and has defined the language of Virgin since its conception. With this in mind, I urge you to scan the Virgin.com website – refreshing and different.

It is probably easier to ask what the Virgin/Branson duo does *not* do. In the words of Virgin themselves, within their "Group Hug" pages on Virgin.com: *"It's a pretty long list, but here goes: travel, media and telecoms, TV, health and fitness, finance, healthcare, drinks, spas, wines, publishing, beauty, experiences, radio, gaming, passenger motorbikes, music and even space tourism. Phew".* Virgin appears to be more experienced than the name may suggest.

Branson is also a founding member of a group known as "The Elders" which aims to find solutions to global problems that create human suffering, and is highly active in other global charities and organisation's supporting initiatives from schools in Africa, through ecology and banning nuclear weapons.

What's interesting about him?

When Branson set up his airline he said *"My interest in life comes from setting myself huge, apparently unachievable challenges and trying to rise above them... from the perspective of wanting to live life to the full, I felt that I had to attempt it".*

It is this visionary orientation that had led to Branson being regarded as a perfect example of a transformational leader, seeking out new challenges and engaging in heroic struggles that support the cause of his organisation. This has led to an organisation which many may regard as bottom heavy but is not suffocated by top line managers. It is based upon informality, information and sharing of common success.

For instance, after a series of legal disputes with British Airways in the 1990's, Branson shared his personal half million pound compensation with his employees, branding this as the "BA bonus".

But it is not just his tendency to seek challenging business opportunities that fascinate. Branson has proven a master at extending his maverick business thinking to his private life, targeting and breaking world records for extreme sports activities such as hot air balloon racing.

Is he an honest leader?

Branson is an enduring entrepreneur, motivational, inspirational, and deeply alluring. Many years ago, when I was working in the marketing department of a UK based airline, I met Branson during one of his home based garden parties. He took the time to personally meet & greet the hundreds of awe inspired twenty something's – I was one of them – and say "hello".

I will not forget his big friendly grin – I instantly liked and warmed to him. Thinking back he struck me as humble and refreshingly "normal", a trait that appears to have kept him out of the bad boy limelight. He acts as if he is "one of the crowd" and this brings instant respect. He oozes trust, authenticity and "niceness".

Branson himself said *"you can't be a good leader if you don't genuinely like people".* He urges praise for a job well done, for this is the best motivator. He is known to rarely fire employees, believing that moving them around to other tasks that better matches their capabilities will bring out their best. *"Look for the best, and you will get the best",* says Branson.

Branson is passionate about doing the right things. He said *"above all you want to create something you are proud of... that is my philosophy of business. I can honestly say that I have never gone into business to make money. If this is the sole motive, then I believe you are better off doing nothing".* I do not know about you, but that nicely makes Branson a top dog in these pages.

This refreshingly different thinking has allowed Virgin, despite many odds, to stand the test of time. Today Virgin group earns some $21 billion around the world and is one of the most respected large "fun" brands.

These leaders are just a tiny handful of examples where honest thinking has been allowed to thrive and has become anchored into corporate culture. All are profitable household names. They help demonstrate that leaders and organisations that follow some moral or honest philosophy will not necessarily suffer in quantitative terms.

The belief was nicely summarised by British Telecom, when in its 1996/7 annual review it introduced a small section entitled "Why are we helping the community: we are all part of the same team". It stated: *"It is becoming increasingly clear that businesses cannot regard themselves as in some way separate from the communities in which they operate. Besides, research has shown that the decision to purchase from one company rather than another is not a decision about price alone".*

Behind many of these organisations stands a leader with an invariably well-formed attitude to morality. Not everyone will agree with them – for example Jobs was seen at times as being paranoid, overly protective and highly critical. Branson is sometimes argued to be a playboy living off the proceeds of a snappy brand name, and racing around the world getting free publicity in unnecessary daredevil stunts. Similarly Wal-Mart is sometimes accused of being a killer of small businesses as it is interested only in its own corporate gain. Despite the criticism, it cannot be denied however, that these leaders have had an impact and have generated impressive financial results in part through following their moral compass.

But why is having a moral compass so important? Is it *really* needed for the proper functioning of the firm? No. There are many organisations that have enjoyed years of high profits and whose leaders do not appear to have any kind of purpose except making money.

Banks spring to mind. Returning to UBS, a company that managed to report around $25 billion revenues in the last years, included an introduction letter from its CEO in its 2011 annual report. This letter is some 2,000 words long – but notably for a company of this size, less than 100, fewer than 5%, relates to people and the community. The absence of moral thinking is so clear, it is almost embarrassing.

But can the CEO be blamed? He is after all operating in a money orientated culture, exemplified by the CSR report of UBS that lacks passion, emotion and inspiration. They state *"corporate responsibility means understanding the concerns and expectations of our stakeholders and integrating these into the decision making process"*. Further: *"Responsible corporate conduct helps create sustainable value for the company"*. Hmm. So what happened to sustainable value for customer? What happened to the employee who contributes to the success of the organisation? Where does society fit? It all seems a bit dry doesn't it? The CEO and the organisation seem to fit like hand in a glove.

UBS leaders are not alone. There are many leaders who are recognised as top achievers but would not necessarily be our first choice as examples of moral thinking. I have already referred to Rupert Murdoch and Adolf Hitler in some detail; but to this pair we can add the likes of Joe Cassano (bringing down AIG); Bernhard Madoff and the leaders of other large companies such as Lehman Brothers, Enron and so on.

Our leaders need to find a balance between achieving results and demonstrating some degree of moral direction. For example, following his masterly rescue of Nissan from near bankruptcy in the late 1990's, the Chairman & CEO of Paris & Tokyo based Renault Nissan, Carlos Ghosn, became known as "le cost killer" and "Mr Fix it". This does not engender the feeling that Ghosn is driven by honest "people orientated" decision-making. He is known as an impatient man of action, for example giving only 48 hours' notice for his handpicked executives to decide whether or not to join him in Tokyo.

He is often regarded as demanding and performance driven – but nevertheless a visionary leader who places communication & people high up on his agenda, encouraging them to achieve the results that are needed. Ghosn said in an interview with CNN *"you have to connect with the people in a company… you have to feel the situation… you have to understand the expectations and have to respond to them"*.

Given all of the above, it would appear that a moral compass is not critical to leadership or organisational success. Both approaches appear to produce positive results. So why is it even important, beyond the few examples we have discussed? Can we ignore the idea that a moral compass adds long-term corporate value? No, that we can't.

Mourkogiannis argued that this is not possible for three reasons. First, morality is today big money. If we can identify and relate to the idea that a moral compass has at least played a part in the return on investment, then the image of the organisation and its leaders will be enhanced. There have been too many Enron's and Parmalats where CEO's and other top figures are imprisoned for fraud. Today, investors and other stakeholders need to feel good that they are "doing the right thing" and backing the right horse.

> *"Morality is today big money. If we can identify and relate to the idea that a moral compass has at least played a part in the return on investment, then the image of the organisation and its leaders will be enhanced"*

Second, having a moral compass reveals the underlying human dynamics of the firm, the most fundamental issues involving motivation and behaviour. It acknowledges that people make up the backbone of most successful companies – not processes. And third, it's the right thing to talk about. If our leaders for example are unable to express and demonstrate a genuine, believable commitment to morality, ethics and society as a whole, the organisation risks being branded as amoral. It becomes the kind of company that professes, "We are here only to make money."

This may work in the short run, but it cannot endure and it is not sustainable. It also creates cynicism amongst employees and investors and risks that the working environment becomes poisoned with miss-trust, eroding innovation, inspiration, motivation, decision-making capabilities and ultimately competitive advantage. Without a moral compass – a strong purpose that followers can unite behind – an organisation will eventually paralyse itself.

And that is the interesting thing. Leaders who are honest – who follow a morality compass – do it because they believe it's the right thing to do. A funny thing happens when leaders consistently act in alignment with their principles and values: they typically produce consistently high performance almost any way you can measure it – gross sales, profits, talent retention, company reputation and customer satisfaction.

Let's consider Apple once again. The Jobs/Apple combo was not always moral, but the very idea of making new, innovative yet simple technologies available to all has been especially powerful. Back in 2009, Tom Cook, CEO of Apple was quoted on CNN Money: *"We believe that we are on the face of the earth to make great products and that's not changing. We are constantly focusing on innovating. We believe in the simple not the complex... we have the self-honesty to admit when we're wrong and the courage to change. And I think, regardless of who is in what job, those values are so embedded in this company that Apple will do extremely well".*

Employees who left, returned. Jobs magnetism, his genius, his charisma, his boldness and his persistence fostered an environment rarely seen in a global organisation – one of courage, oneness and entrepreneurship. The focus provided Apple the collective courage and persistence to strike out from the pack. And that approach has supported its meteoric rise in the last decade and achieving a market capitalisation higher than the GDP of some *countries*.

It's a similar story at Starbucks. The long serving CEO Harold Schutz writes in the introductory pages to the 2011 annual report: *"I still believe that shareholder value must be linked to creating value for a company's people, value for its customers and – perhaps now more than ever – value for the communities it serves. Balancing profitability and social conscience is as much a part of Starbucks' core as coffee".*

Visit any store or website and you'll see colourful posters proudly showing pictures of coffee pickers in Africa or some other far flung destination. They tout the company's fair trade coffees, charitable donations and other feel good things to do with coffee and the communities they serve. Their annual report discusses the benefits they provide to employees, such as stock options, tuition and health care – and as a result investors feel like they are backing a responsible company, consumers that they have a positive impact on the world when drinking their coffee and employees a sense of pride that they are adding value to the community whilst being fairly rewarded for their work.

According to Harald Schutz *"consumers will embrace only the companies and brands they trust and with which they identify…. The approach Starbucks is committed to is the only one that will enable us to deliver long-term value to shareholders, partners and customers".* And with this background the company posted record gross revenues of $13.3 billion in 2012 and earnings per share up 10% to $1.79.

It is becoming clear that following an effective, meaningful moral compass is more than a PR stunt. It is not a means to an end, but it is the means in itself. If it is treated as an underhand way to enhance image and make money, then it will not work. A moral compass must be first be lived and breathed by top management in an organisation as they are the only ones who can influence corporate culture change.

And one way of spreading the moral word throughout an organisation and to its external stakeholders is through corporate social responsibility (CSR). CSR refers to corporate conscience, corporate citizenship and self-responsibility. It's about the ethics that an organisation is prepared to stand by. It is "bigger" than a leader and is, indirectly, about the whole organisation being "honest" and reflecting moral ideals initiated by top management. CSR is a process that aims to embrace responsibility for the company's actions and encourage a positive impact through its activities on the environment, consumers, employees, communities and other stakeholders.

It is not a balance sheet entry, but a self-regulating mechanism that ensures organisational self-compliance with the spirit of the law, international standards and things that are accepted as being morally "right". In this respect CSR can be regarded as the mechanism that guides corporations, its top decision makers and its employees on moral issues. It's an honesty guide. Proponents of CSR argue that corporates can be more profitable in the long run by operating with the moral and honest perspective that is discovered within CSR.

Victoria Lopez and two colleagues studied the financial performance of 110 companies between 1999 and 2004. Half followed the principles of the Dow Jones Sustainability Index (corporate social responsibility) and the other half were not members. The (DJSI) was created in 1999 to track the stock performance of the world's leading companies in terms of economic, environmental and social criteria.

They found that after a short term negative impact (investments in new processes and practices under CSR) firms that had embraced corporate social responsibility had higher gross profit margins and higher returns on assets and equity than those that didn't.

To explain the socially conscious businesses' economic success, the economists cited enhanced levels of loyalty and trust among their customers, especially those deemed "morally conscious". This indicates that following a moral compass or instigating some kind of CSR approach contributes positively to the bottom line, by making multiple stakeholders think more positively towards the firm and helping engender loyalty.

In an early attempt to demonstrate this link, James Burke, the former CEO of Johnson & Johnson, compiled a list of companies with a record of ethics and social thinking, including 3M, IBM, Coca-Cola, J&J etc. He found that these organisations grew at an average annual rate of 11.3% compared to the 6.2% recorded by the Dow Jones index of companies between 1950 and 1990.

Burke ascribes this benefit to the fact that CSR policies made the public more willing to consider businesses' point of view, strengthened the businesses' information structure with society, made it easier for the business to motivate and recruit employees and added value to its products and services.

Burke is certainly not a lone voice arguing the business case for CSR. A study by Verschoor and Murphy entitled "best corporate citizens have best financial performance" considered the 100 "Best corporate citizens" of 2001 (according to parameters established by KLD, an independent organisation assessing corporate social performance of S&P 500 companies) and compared them to the financial performance of the rest of the S&P 500. It found that those top 100 organisations performed at least 10 percentage points better than those outside the list.

"If people are not inspired and do not see its value, strategy may well falter"

But it takes more than an honest leader and a robust CSR approach to be successful. Great leaders also understand that the success of a strategy depends partly upon the level of emotional support that the strategy attracts from different levels of the organisation. If people are not inspired and do not see its value, strategy may well falter. Thus, successful strategies must be shaped by a good dose of both *"what"* and *"why"* – otherwise employees and customers will struggle to optimise the thinking and embed this into everyday thought. Without a "why", leaders will fail in the long run to anchor change with followers.

BMW is one organisation that has managed to successfully marry corporate strategies with employee and customer engagement. By the end of the 20th century, it was a fiercely independent organisation that was exceptionally successful at building the "*ultimate driving machine*", and had spent the better part of 50 years carefully nurturing its image as a builder of fine performance orientated cars.

The whole idea of efficiency, economy and downsizing was arguably as alien as speaking Swahili in the German dominated management board. It laughed at the idea of building small cars; it denounced the thought of front wheel drive and had built an excellent reputation for engineering that was centred on its straight six cylinder engines. They were successful, profitable and enjoyed customer and employee loyalty that bordered on fanaticism.

However, leadership recognised early on the need for change, and with global indicators pointing towards transparency, sustainability, corporate responsibility, moral thinking, vehicle downsizing and rising oil costs, the management committee took the BMW Group against the grain of its traditional thinking and in 2001 launched a small front wheel drive car and called it MINI. To help employees understand the "why" they launched internal Brand Behaviour programmes and other culture changing initiatives.

Loyalists shuddered, but the company remained true to its core strategy. The "new" MINI remained "premium", but represented a sweeping change in thinking and engineering for the boffins in Munich. It was everything a BMW wasn't. But it was a resounding success, selling more than 200,000 units within a few years on the market and in 2012 topping 300,000 for the first time.

BMW followed this in 2007 with its first sustainability report. It stated: "*Within the BMW Group, sustainability is... not the responsibility of an individual department or a particular division. Instead, it starts off in the minds of all its employees and culminates, day after day, in the results that those employees achieve for the company.*" In the following years BMW followed with various initiatives that created clear visibility for the organisation. On the strategic side it announced "Number ONE" a five-year plan outlining four key focus areas, covering not only business efficiencies, but also customers and technologies.

On the product side, "efficient dynamics", initially conceived in 2000, was publicly launched as a clear communications and engineering strategy. This has reduced the emissions of its vehicles by 30% since 1995 and will continue to be central theme in its drive for greater efficiencies when new electric vehicles come on stream in the near future. Business processes now include environmental and sustainable targets, which are also published in its annual reports. Today, the strategy is winning international recognition – the Group has been a leader on the Dow Jones Sustainability Index since 2005.

What has made BMW so successful? They managed to frame their moral compass into an inspirational set of actions that was also embedded into corporate strategy. It was not just an idea on paper and communicated by accident at the back of their website, but was reflected in every action the company made, from business processes, decision making and product development through to engineering expertise, communication and leadership decisions. Employees lived it. Customers bought it. Investors supported it. It is in their DNA.

As Mourkogiannis argues, *"the individual who aspires to be a leader must throw off traditional typecast roles: the wealthy entrepreneur or investor, the famous deal maker, the tough chief executive, even the charismatic leader. These roles have become commodities — they can be adopted at will by individuals… the true business leader's more significant role is to be in touch with, and act on, the moral currents that influence… People do not want commoditised leadership; they want principles. To fulfil this role requires understanding of the moral issues"*.

The last pages, I believe, illustrate that moral thinking and honest leadership offers quantitative pay back. But what is the impact from a qualitative perspective?

THE QUALITATIVE VIEW

We cannot avoid the need for quantitative results. It's a fact of modern life. The good news is that the bottom line can be positively influenced by "moral, honest thinking", whether this is represented in the hearts, minds and actions of influential leaders like Richard Branson or J&J's Burke or is wrapped up in a Corporate Social Responsibility programme at the organisational level. But the same approach can also add value from a different "softer" perspective.

By that I do not mean banal "miscellaneous items", but things such as corporate reputation, employee trust, employee engagement and retention, employee health, a sense of belonging (organisational community) and so on.

We all know that happy people make more money; they work harder and smile longer. Equally, happy customers will come back for more. The challenge however, is that most of these things do not have a position on the balance sheet and that makes them less interesting to our leaders, as they must demonstrate measurable added value to outside investing stakeholders. No balance sheet entry means no measurable value and the idea of "doing things right" does not always win friends on the trading floor.

The closest thing we can arguably find on a balance sheet is "goodwill" – but this entry is often used to refer to such things as brand equity for example. This supports the idea that some brands have grown so valuable that they have gained their own marketplace momentum and customers may even make a purchase because of the power of the brand rather than the product they actually get.

For example, do you buy the brand or the product Coca-Cola? They have become one and the same. Do you go for a McDonalds or a burger? Do you drink a coffee or a Starbucks? The brand has gained a perceived value that has become so high that it and not necessarily the products can generate customer loyalty. Investors wish to reflect this brand value on the balance sheet.

Unfortunately this is not the case with being able to offer consumers happy people and thrilled communities – they do not (yet) make the balance sheet as a profit or loss entry because they will not always generate sufficient revenue.

But will this always be true? I believe we are beginning to see evidence of a shift in thinking from potential consumers that can influence loyalty beyond the power of a brand. Consumers also want to be associated to the right companies with a great reputation for moral thinking, and this can move brands more quickly than just a strong name.

Take for instance the launch of the then new Toyota Prius back in the late 1990's. As a product it was not especially competitive compared to similar sized vehicles at the time. The only stand out feature was its unique drivetrain and low emissions. But it was launched at the right time, when California stipulated that 5% of all new cars sold had to be low emissions and other governments were discussing increasing car taxation on high emission vehicles. Such considerations therefore quickly moved to the forefront of consumer minds and they looked for alternatives that moved them away from other automotive brands.

Consequently, even though the brand Toyota does not exactly excite, the car became a cult, therefore moving the brand into an area not held by any other mainstream manufacturer at the time. Toyota was elevated onto an "environmental brand" pedestal that it retains and leads today.

We know that an honest and moral approach does influence the reputation of our leaders and their organisations. Think about it – would you go to a dentist or doctor if they had a dodgy reputation? Probably not. Equally, when you booked your last vacation, did you check websites such as tripadvisor.com to check out the experiences of past travellers? Or when you purchased your last car, did you do it without chatting to anyone else other than your sales person? In fact, think about the majority of your purchases – they are based on experience, hearsay, direct information or recommendation – in other words the reputation that surrounds the product, brand, organisation or even the leaders will influence your decision to purchase.

Many organisations consider their greatest asset to be their good name or intellectual property (IP). This is especially the case for knowledge-based organisations and consultancy services, such as medical, legal, learning & development and so on. Knowledge is their

IP – without it they have nothing to sell. And for them to be able to sell their knowledge, they need a watertight reputation.

Leaders and organisations that have managed to build a great reputation often discover that they have created an unspoken ability to charge premium prices, to secure support for controversial decisions from stakeholders, to help support organisation value and share prices and to gain more loyalty from both customers and employees. A great reputation has enabled them to generate an informal aura of "trust" within its supply & value chain that people want to be associated with.

But is having "just" a great reputation enough? No, because leaders should also be aware that reputation is one of the fastest moving aspects of corporate "value" – it is exceptionally volatile, and it is often taken for granted until it becomes threatened by some dramatic event or shift in values.

Following the Deepwater Horizon oil spill in 2010 for instance, BP experienced a dramatic and sudden reduction in its reputation. According to branddirectory.com the BP brand rating fell from AA+ to BB in the 12 months following the accident. This was combined with 28% decrease in brand value to $8.7 billion. As Warren Buffet aptly said: *"It takes 20 years to build a reputation – and five minutes to ruin it"*. Managing reputation therefore requires both an understanding of its parameters and a method of measuring changes within those parameters.

There are a number of methods that have been used over the years to measure reputation, the results published annually in reports such as Fortunes AMAC (Americas Most Admired Companies), the Financial Times "Worlds (Europe's) Most Respected Companies", Management Today's "Britain's most respected companies" and the Delahaye Medialink: "Corporate Reputation Index". Even more complex economic measurements such as the Harris-Fonbrum reputation quotient (RQ) add to the growing pile of devices that allow our leaders to identify the drivers, their components and check progress of corporate reputation. Drivers of reputation may typically include:

Emotional Appeal/Ethical: We have a good feeling about the company. We admire, respect and trust it.

Employees/Vision/Leadership/Workplace: We believe in the company and that its leaders encourage and develop talent, have a clear vision, see opportunities and appear to respect employees.

Products & Services: We feel that the company and its leaders stand behind their products and services, they are innovative and fairly priced and of high quality.

Social responsibility: We see that the organisation and its leaders communicate and share ideas about their contribution to the community such as social funding and trusts, and is seen to actively communicate the sustainability values.

Financial performance: We are comfortable that the organisation has a good profitability record that is not too volatile with good prospects.

Customer focus: We believe the company is customer and not product centric and that its leaders consider the needs of customers before other stakeholders, and that they understand the importance of loyalty.

Given the above, it is clear that any attempt to calculate the financial value of reputation will be challenging to say the least. Perhaps a better question is why a measurement is even needed? After all, reputation is largely based on ethical thinking and no one will bet against a change in ethics. We have learned that leaders can add a lot to reputation and our intuition should already be able to give us some hints – what, I wonder, would the value of Virgin be without Richard Branson, or where would Apple be today without the influence of Steve Jobs?

From many respects a good reputation is an asset and a bad one is a liability. But as this is hard to quantify, the best way to express it is through narrative methods, such as a corporate social responsibility report. But this is, when done properly, a significant undertaking. CSR reporting should be treated with the same degree of rigorousness as, say, financial reporting.

That means, CSR reports that are essentially designed to support corporate reputation should include detailed indicators, benchmarks, targets and trends, as well as case studies. This will add a degree of credibility to the activities and help overcome potential scepticism from stakeholders, internal and external. And once underway, CSR approaches need to set the objectives for both current and future values in order to aid investors, employees, management and other stakeholders.

The BP Group has arguably become the most explicitly environmentally oriented large oil company following the Deepwater Horizon incident referred to above. Combined with its loss of reputation, it also suffered an astonishing 79% drop in enterprise value within 12 months, to "just" $152 billion. In addition it took a $41 billion hit in pre-tax charges for compensation claims and clean up, lost over four million barrels of oil to sea and made other financial commitments in environmental research. This all clearly left an indelible mark.

So much so that Bob Dudley, the new Chief Executive of the BP Group stated in his sustainability report letter: *"We have set three clear priorities – safety must be enhanced, trust earned back and greater value delivered to our shareholders. We know we don't have all the answers, but we will keep learning and striving for continuous improvement. We will do our best to keep you informed".* The leaders of the Group have now created a clear visibility chain for its sustainable reporting and taken steps to have this accredited by Ernst & Young.

It reports on achievements that cover over 35 performance indicators across four key pillars including Safety, People, Environment and Performance. These indicators include such diverse topics as greenhouse gas emissions, number of oil spills, employee injury days and women in leadership. It reports on subcontractor work, joint ventures, stakeholder engagement and even includes a case studies library. But it took the "dramatic event" to push BP to this level.

Professor Charles Fombrun, research professor of management at the Stern School of Business, New York University, believes that *"a reputation develops from a company's uniqueness and from identity-shaping practices, maintained over time, that lead stakeholders to perceive the company as credible, reliable, responsible and trustworthy…. Best regarded companies achieve their reputations by systematically practicing mundane management. They adhere rigorously to practices that consistently and reliably produce decisions that the rest of us approve of and respect. By increasing our faith and confidence in the company's actions, credibility and reliability create economic value".*

This would point to experience and information as being key sources of reputation. The former comes from past dealings that a customer, employee or other stakeholder has had. This may be a direct experience or could even be indirectly spread through word of mouth amongst a group of friends for example.

The latter is driven through a consistent internal and external PR, via every possible channel to every possible stakeholder. It is not only done by producing an attractive CSR document and calling it a day. It needs more. That means values, strategies, processes, visions and missions must reflect the image of the organisation. And the decisions and activities of leaders must be aligned.

And this approach is working at BP. According to the same source, (branddirectory.com) the brand rating of BP as of end 2011 had improved from the BB following the accident back up to an A, and its brand value has steadily risen by $1.5 billion to $10.2 billion. Clearly this is still way below performance prior to the accident and it will take some time to restore its reputation, but the integrated approach appears to be paying dividends.

Johnson & Johnson – An honest organisation?

Who are they?

J&J was founded in 1886 and is today one of the largest and most diverse companies in the world. It operates in 3 primary sectors – consumer products, medical devices and pharmaceuticals. It is the world's sixth largest healthcare company, the largest medical devices and diagnostics company and the eighth largest pharmaceutical company. At the last count they are made up of more than 250 operating companies across 60 countries and employ around 129,000 people.

They are behind many famous household products such as Listerine, Band Aids, baby powder, Neutrogena skin products and of course the famous Tylenol which ended up costing it $100 million in recall costs but cemented its brand reputation for moral thinking.

Are they successful?

Of course, size alone does not guarantee success, but despite a dip during the crisis years of 2009 and 2010, the organisation still reports sales revenues in the region of $63 billion, net earnings of around $10 billion and earnings per share at approximately $3.50 – relatively consistent year after year for the past several years. You can decide for yourself if this is "success" or not.

What makes them remarkable?

Their Credo, which is consistently and religiously applied, helps make J&J stand out from the crowd. One insider says of J&J "*it is a really great company to work for, and the people in general are the cream of the crop as far as integrity, values and work ethic*" [are concerned].

The organisations Credo, dating back to 1943, is the moral bedrock of J&J. The ideal "putting people we serve first" was sorely tested back in 1982 when someone laced the Tylenol medication with cyanide, killing seven people. At the time, Tylenol had 35% market share for over the counter pain killers. Its market share collapsed to around 7% after the poisoning incident.

J&J's handling of the crisis remains an example of moral thinking. It recalled over 31 million bottles of the product, an exercise that cost in excess of $100 million. In a 2004 Wharton School Publishing Book titled "Lasting Leadership": "*What You Can Learn from the Top 25 Business People of Our Times*", James Burke, ex CEO of J&J emphasised the value of the J&J Credo: "*The Credo is all about the consumer*", Burke said. When those seven deaths occurred "*the Credo made it very clear at that point exactly what we were all about. It gave me the ammunition I needed to persuade shareholders and others to spend the $100 million on the recall. The Credo helped sell it*".

It even stopped making the product for a short time; found temporary jobs for its employees and it showed video-taped reports to its employees explaining how it was handling the crisis. This imbued a sense of pride and purpose into its followers. An employee who joined in the 1990's, long after the episode, said: "*It became a part of the culture. They thought, we do things right, we do things well. I do not think I've ever worked in a place where everybody was so tough on themselves*".

All actions were on the initiative of the company, which helped preserve its reputation as reflected in the Credo. And it enabled a gradual comeback of Tylenol albeit with new packaging and tamper proof seals.

Today the Credo is embedded into every strand of the organisation and crucially aligned with its strategy. Consistency remains at the core of its responsibility approach, from which it has not wavered for 70 years. Its 82 page responsibility report starts and ends with the philosophies of the company Credo.

As Alex Gorsky states in his introductory letter to the report: "*Johnson & Johnson is a company that does good and does well. This is the simplest expression of how we live up to the principles of our Credo*". J&J is one of the most iconic and trusted brands – the one whose products you would give to your children.

Does this approach win recognition?

The consistent commitment of J&J to follow its Credo has earned the company a number of awards. For instance it has been ranked No. 2 by Interbrand's 2012 Best Global Green Brands report; it was named to *Fortune* magazine's list of the World's Most Admired Companies in 2011 and in the same year it received a perfect score of 100% for the seventh consecutive year on the annual Corporate Equality Index (CEI) established by the Human Rights Campaign Foundation (HRC).

Even The United Nations bestowed its 2011 Humanitarian of the Year Award for J&J's leading role in its Healthy Mother, Healthy Child initiative; it continues to be a member company of the FTSE4Good Index and even *Working Mother* magazine has named Johnson & Johnson one of the "Top 100 Companies for Working Mothers" every year since the list was initiated 26 years ago.

Trust is one of the drivers of corporate reputation and an integral element in CSR, but it is also one of the major contributions to employee morale and so called employee engagement. I believe that a working environment that encourages trustworthy exchange between employees and leaders will, if done properly, enhance employee engagement, talent retention, performance and wellbeing.

James Burke, the ex CEO of J&J agrees. He noted in the Wharton Book "Lasting Leadership: What You Can Learn from the Top 25 Business People of Our Times", *"Trust has been an operative word in my life. [It] embodies almost everything you can strive for that will help you to succeed. You tell me any human relationship that works without trust, whether it is a marriage or a friendship or a social interaction; in the long run, the same thing is true about business"*.

Nevertheless, despite the wise words of great leaders, a Kenexa WorkTrends survey in 2011 found that trust levels are declining, and confidence in senior management is going down the toilet. Less than half of surveyed employees (48%) trusted their managers, with 28% actively distrusting managers and 24% remaining undecided. The Maritz Institute recorded similar findings: in 2010 & 2011 it found that one fifth of its Employee Values survey respondents have no faith in their leadership and do not feel their leaders can be trusted and that they are not honest and ethical.

Scandals such as Enron, WorldCom and Tyco and threats of layoffs and downsizing have only exacerbated the problem. *"In times like these, trust is an especially critical issue. Companies need their best people more than ever to be engaged and productive. But often, this process starts at the top"*, says Rick Garlick Ph.D., senior director of consulting and strategic implementation at Maritz. *"You've got to maintain credibility with your workforce as a means of getting them to totally buy in to the mission and vision of your company. Anything less fosters a disengaged workforce that puts self-interest at the top of its list of priorities."*

And this has remarkable implications for employee engagement. For example, having surveyed more than 1,000 workers across different industries, Maritz found that

- Only 45% of employees said they feel rewarded and recognised by their employers.
- Of the 55% who did not feel recognised for their efforts, 80% did not feel completely satisfied with their job.
- Of those who did not feel recognised, 58% did not feel motivated to go beyond their normal job duties to get the job done.
- 33% identified themselves as employees who just "stay the course" rather than being motivated to make a difference.

Further, the research found that contrary to our popular belief that we are all just happy to have a job, disengaged workers were staying longer than they did in 2006. But while disengaged employees are staying longer, top performers, the important corporate talent, moved on faster, and it is estimated that around 25% would leave if the chance was available.

So what does this mean? First and foremost in low trust organisations employee disengagement will occur. These employees have become disconnected, feel underutilised, are skeptical and may present a contagious negativity that damages the working atmosphere. Especially critical is that this disengaged group shows a loyalty (they are not leaving!) that an organisation may not wish to encourage.

The global consultancy firm Blessing White in its 2011 Global Engagement Report argued that disengaged employees often *"stay for what they can get"* – job security, bonuses, good salaries and even career advancement after they replace the top dogs who have left.

This may not seem like a big deal until it is understood that it is not the good ones who stay. They run off, meaning many organisations maybe left with the so called B&C performers and very few top dogs. I think that this is highly damaging to innovation, motivation and the organisations capacity for transformational thinking – and therefore by implication the ability to move an organisation forward.

Consider for example the impact on your organisation if your best sales person was to leave. Or what would happen if the most committed and popular leader was to leave. What about the CIO, the top HR person or most experienced R&D expert? It is not just the loss of the person and cost of recruiting a replacement. It is the cost of loss experience and especially knowledge.

More often than not this knowledge is implicit – it is not written down or stored on a server – it's in the employees mind, and if they go, it is no longer accessible to you. And if these people are your best, what are you left with? Only the second best – which is not really what most of us want.

Therefore, creating a culture of trust becomes increasingly important – but much like the efforts needed to create a positive reputation, it is not a walk in the park. Some years ago global employee retention firm, TalentKeepers surveyed over 40,000 workers across 350 organisations, and whilst the survey is a little old, it remains as valid today as a decade ago. It found that competitive pay, benefits and typical HR programmes, while helpful, were insufficient in generating trust and employee retention.

"Most workers, particularly those on the front line where it really matters, feel as though leaders have ultimate power in the workplace – power over pay, promotions, favourable assignments, job security and more. People's satisfaction, productivity and engagement hinge most on someone who treats them fairly and whom they can trust" says Richard Finnegan, Chief Client Services Officer for TalentKeepers. Finnegan adds: *"Responsibility and accountability for retaining talent needs to move out to the front lines and into the hands of leaders... being a trust builder consistently surfaces as what employees most desire and expect of their immediate leader".*

According to organisational scientists, trust has become a combination of three core determinants:

- Competence (Can they do the job?)
- Benevolence (Do they care about me?)
- Integrity (Are they honest?)

These three combined account for about 80% of the factors that drive trust in leaders. Any leader wishing to generate trust in their followers need to be able to demonstrate all three elements.

Yet, some of these qualities are more important than others. Integrity for example scored highest importance in the Kenexa survey at 41%, with competence last at 25%. Therefore, when the goal is to maximise trust, leaders must know how to do their jobs well, but it is even more important for them to be kind and honest with their employees. This begins when one person opens up to another, and it must be leaders who start the trust process. Leaders earn trust by showing that they have the competence, the knowledge, the personality, the systems, the frameworks and the processes necessary to make people feel safe and trusting.

This trust creates energy and a higher acceptability of risk. Leaders must therefore not only talk about their ethical values, they must live those values and walk the talk.

Hector Ruiz, CEO of AMD in an interview with Forbes Magazine in 2005 said *"Surround yourself with people of integrity and get out of their way. In my adult years as a manager, Bob Galvin, the former CEO of Motorola, was my most influential leader. He told me: 'A good leader knows he is doing a good job when he knows with certainty that he can say yes to anything his staff asks and feels totally confident that they will do the right thing'. If you surround yourself with the right people who have integrity, and they all understand well the goals and objectives of the organisation, then the best thing to do as a leader is to get out of their way. I use this advice quite a bit at work. The right people will feel far more pressure to perform well when they are trusted".*

But the responsibility also falls on the company and especially it's CEO to encourage an environment for all leaders to practice trust. A CEO cannot just endorse a set of moral values and have a bunch of posters and screen savers produced and expect us to follow them. The values have to be demonstrated in processes, practices and actions otherwise they remain only good in intentions.

> *"A CEO cannot just endorse a set of moral values and have a bunch of posters and screen savers produced and expect employees to follow them"*

This might include a CEO visibly getting behind mission statements, employee opinion surveys, quality improvement initiatives, customer satisfaction processes, yearly performance reviews and cross-training of employees to name a few best practices. Organisations that engage in these established methods have more employees who trust their leaders.

According to Kenexa, the odds that an employee trusts senior leadership doubles, if the organisation uses one of the ideas in the past paragraph. Moreover use all of these best practices, and the odds an employee trusts leadership are six times higher than in organisations that do not engage in any best practices.

This impacts employee and talent retention. If trust levels are high, individuals are more likely to stay; Maritz for example, found that those of us who consider that we are consistently recognised in ways that are meaningful to us, are 11 times more likely to spend our career with the company and seven times more likely to feel completely satisfied with our job.

However, the question that may interest many senior HR leaders: "*Is the company successful because of engaged employees*" or "*are employees engaged because the organisation is so successful*" has not really been effectively answered. Blessing Whitehouse interviewed one female executive of a Fortune 500 financial services firm who maintained that she was able to demonstrate higher performance in high engagement areas, but was not able to confirm causation – yet.

In its Global Engagement Report, Blessing White discusses other organisations that have conducted landmark research espousing the business case for trust and employee engagement. Some of the more recent findings it discusses include those of Gallup "*organisations with comparatively high proportions of engaged employees were much less likely than the rest to see a decline in EPS in 2008, the year after the recession began*". Or Hewitt Associates "*high engagement firms had total shareholder return that was 19% higher than average in 2009. In low engagement organisations, it's 44% below average*".

Despite the lack of causation, it has become accepted that in progressive, trust based organisations there is a return. Pat Hasbrook, Senior Vice President for Experian, a Fortune 500 financial information firm, when interviewed by Blessing White for its Global Engagement Survey said "*we simply accept the premise that an engaged workforce is essential to the success of the company*".

According to Kenexa in its WorkTrends survey "Trust Matters", the linkages between trust and employee behaviour go beyond employee engagement and turnover however. The WorkTrends research shows that trust in leadership may also be important to employee well-being and health. Employees who distrust their leaders are seven times more likely to report they are mentally and physically unwell. We all know that healthy people mean fewer sick days, and depending on the organisational set up and local regulations, fewer sick days can also mean lower insurance costs for health care schemes and accidents. This means more contribution to the bottom line.

This is because employees who distrust their leaders are more likely to be stressed at work. In fact, the WorkTrends report notes that amongst those of us who trust our leadership only 13% report unreasonable stress, compared to 62% if we distrust our leaders. Another interesting review was published in Psychology Today. This summarised a survey made by Jaana Kuoppala, Anne Lamminpää, Juha Liira and Harri Vaino. They looked at 109 different studies linking workplace leadership to the well-being of those being led.

> "Lower anxiety and stress levels are recorded when employees felt considered and part of a trusted environment"

The researchers focused on leadership styles that encompassed consideration and support. A considerate leader is one who treats us kindly and fairly. A supportive leader is one who treats us with concern and provides encouragement. In other words they focused on leaders who think and work ethically and morally – an honest leader. Wellbeing was assessed in various ways: job satisfaction, job well-being (defined as burn-out, exhaustion, anxiety, depression or stress), amount of sick leave and finally early retirement due to disability.

In all cases, positive relationships were found between honest leadership and our wellbeing. The more honest the leader, the healthier we are. The robustness of effects ranged from small to moderate. But even small effects, multiplied over thousands or millions of workers, imply that the impact of "good" leadership on employee wellbeing is potentially staggering.

This finding is aligned to that of the summer 2012 edition of the Employee Outlook survey conducted by the British Chartered Institute of Personnel and Development (BCIPD). The BCIPD demonstrated that there is a link between the trust employees have concerning their senior managers and their personal well-being.

When measuring anxiety levels for example, and ssing a ranking scale of 1 – 10, with 1 being the lowest score, employees who strongly agreed that they trusted their senior management scored a rate of just 2.8 when asked how anxious they felt (i.e. they were not anxious). In contrast the anxiety score jumped to 4.9 for those employees who strongly disagreed that they trusted senior management. The BCIPD said: *"There is a particularly strong link between employees who strongly agree they trust their senior managers and lower than average levels of anxiety".*

When employees were asked to rank anxiety levels according to whether they believed or not they were consulted on decisions by senior management, similar data was attained. In other words, a lower anxiety and stress level is recorded when employees felt considered and part of a trusted environment. The levels of anxiety rose when employees' felt ignored and closed out from this trust based environment.

According to the BCIPD: *"It is in employers' interest to be interested in the well-being of their staff – not just because they have a duty of care towards them – but because of the link between well-being and employee engagement, as well as lower risks of accidents and lower levels of stress and absence".*

I believe it is now clear that a well-chosen moral purpose, one that resonates with the sensibility of customers, employees and other stakeholders contributes at both the quantitative and qualitative level to corporate reputation, employee engagement, a culture of trust and employee well-being.

In turn, this establishes a sense of community and common meaning which is grounded in mutual respect – we know that in these environments we share more than just a "common cause". We also share a sense of teamwork, alignment with leadership and organisational values, a positive work attitude and greater organisational commitment.

In providing a degree of emotional certainty, a well-grounded moral purpose also counters the natural risk aversion of a large company, which might otherwise hold back innovation. It inspires people to search out solutions to problems, to not give up, to keep on trying.

This is something that Alfred P. West Jr., founder and CEO of SEI Investments, realised and lives. SEI is a financial services firm that operates the back-office services for mutual funds. West ditched his nice big corner office usually reserved for the top dogs and joined the pack in the open space. He had all furniture put on wheels and the idea is that all employees are encouraged to move around and secure a clear line of sight to management and to feel part of a wider, transparent community.

When asked why, West says *"The CEO sets the tone for an organisation's culture. If you separate yourself from everybody else with corporate aircraft and enormous stock options, your employees are going to get the wrong message"*. The small firm that began in the 1960's in Oaks, Pennsylvania now operates nine global offices and manages or administers assets to the tune of $448 billion – so not a corner shop with a nice moral policy, but a serious global player.

Southwest Airlines may not be a global player but they are seriously big in the US aviation market. In fact, it's the largest US based airline and the world's largest operator of Boeing 737 aircraft, its fleet in excess of 570 aircraft.

Since its foundation in 1967, it carved out a niche as a low cost carrier that concentrated on giving customers a great deal. Its mission is *"dedication to the highest quality of customer service delivered with a sense of warmth, friendliness, individual pride and company spirit"*. And for the employees *"We are committed to provide our Employees a stable work environment with equal opportunity for learning and personal growth. Creativity and innovation are encouraged for improving the effectiveness of Southwest Airlines. Above all, Employees will be provided the same concern, respect, and caring attitude within the Organisation that they are expected to share externally with every Southwest Customer."*

Starting out of Dallas Love airfield, "LUV" has become an integrated component in its communication: prettiest flight attendants, tickets issued from Love machines and Love bites on board. Even the airlines stock market symbol is LUV. Gary Kelly, Southwest CEO states *"Our people are our single greatest strength and most enduring long term competitive advantage"*.

The culture is very much people orientated, one in which people are seen as a part of a Southwest "family". Even the company annual report describes its Southwest family as having a *"warrior spirit, a servant's heart and a fun loving attitude"*. It's hard not to be a part of the family as an employee. And this spirit pays off. Today, Southwest has over 46,000 employees, and in 2012 reported record gross revenues of $17 billion and 40 consecutive years of profitability. Not bad for a company based around family, trust and love.

These two examples illustrate that leaders of all backgrounds and in all sorts of companies can generate a sense of belonging which in turn can lead to corporate success. It is not rocket science, it can be as simple as sitting or walking amongst employees to engender a team spirit and a sense of belonging. This should be possible in any sized organisation.

So where can we start? We know it's worthwhile, and we know honesty pays. So how do we become a trusted leader and in my view, a top dog? We need answers, and that is the job of Part IV.

PART IV
FINDING THE ANSWERS

"The real leader has no need to lead –
he is content to point the way."
– Henry Miller

"No legacy is so rich as honesty."
– William Shakespeare

"If you're not the lead dog, the view never changes."
– Unknown

In the past, it was believed that "honesty, integrity and following a moral compass" did not need to be listed as a value of leadership. It was just simply a by-product that leaders had as a result of "being human". In the last century, Albert Camus a French philosopher wrote (and we believed), *"Integrity has no need for rules"*. But today things are different.

As we discovered in Part I people (we) lie. Some of us conceal, cheat and hide the truth. We manipulate and falsify. And as a result the emphasis that customers, investors, employees and other stakeholders place on trust is increasing. We see and need guidelines, CSR, sustainability, missions, visions and values as the backbone of organisational and leadership thinking. And it appears that this pays off, both, in the financial markets and in the hearts and minds of the people these activities serve.

In their book "Leaders: The Strategies for Taking Charge", Warren Bennis and Burt Nanus cite trust as a key element of effective leadership: *"Trust is the emotional glue that binds followers and leaders together. The accumulation of trust is a measure of the legitimacy of leadership. It cannot be mandated or purchased; it must be earned. Trust is the basic ingredient of all organisations, the lubrication that maintains the organisation".*

If Bennis and Nanus are correct, then our leaders must shoulder an enormous responsibility: They must establish cultures where trust exists in both directions, from their employees to themselves and vice versa. These cultures must be cascaded into the organisations they lead; it must become the lifeblood and beating heart. And above all, it must start with the themselves. As Shakespeare once lamented, *"to thine own self be true".*

But how? I have put together a simple process that you can follow – the Eight Axioms of Honest Leadership. And to assist you with the internalisation and optimisation of these axioms I have provided some anchoring ideas. Finally, no tool is of value if we cannot track our success – therefore I have also provided some ideas to help you measure your progress, these being collated in an "Honestometer".

Eight Axioms of Honest Leadership

I can imagine that right now some of you maybe asking yourself what on earth I may mean when I refer to the Eight Axioms of Honest Leadership. For those of you who may be a little perturbed by the odd sounding approach, do not fear, this is not at all complex! Rather, it is a simple method that I have designed to help you recall the different traits and behaviours that are linked to honest leadership and we have already discussed in Part II.

The first thing we need to fix is our understanding of an "axiom". An axiom is a starting point of reasoning or a premise. For example, "*our planet is not a square*", or "*1*1 = 1*". But the special thing about an axiom is that regardless of whether this starting point is a word or a statement, it is said to be so *self-evident that it is accepted to be true without any controversy*.

In simpler words, it is taken for granted as being something for which we *do not need proof*. We already know it to be true. The most common use of axioms is to test mathematical theories. A starting point may be "*when an equal amount is taken from two equals, the result will be an equal amount*". Now it does not matter which way you cut this, it is fact. Undeniable truth. Similarly, others will say "*The whole is greater than the part*". This is also true.

Therefore, for our purposes having a set of axioms to help us on our journey makes sense. When you question yourself about the validity of these axioms towards honest leadership you know they are already true. So do not waste your time asking "*if*", rather spend it asking "*how and when*". You already know the why: it's the right thing to do.

So, let's take a look at the axioms in my model. In this case I have collated the traits and behaviours of what I believe make up an honest leader and grouped them together into similar headings, each of which represents one axiom. Numbered from one to eight, these further combine into the easy to recall acronym, FIDELITY:

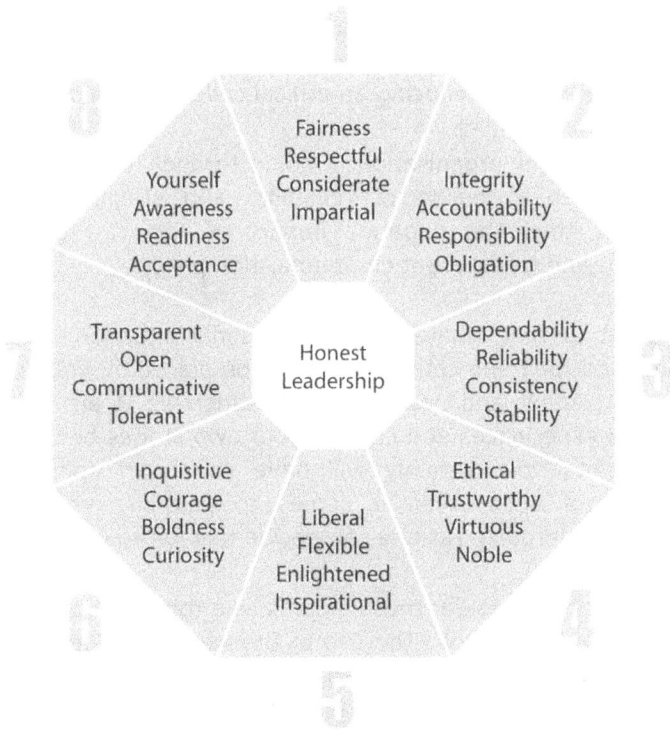

Fairness
Respectful
Considerate
Impartial

Yourself
Awareness
Readiness
Acceptance

Integrity
Accountability
Responsibility
Obligation

Transparent
Open
Communicative
Tolerant

Honest
Leadership

Dependability
Reliability
Consistency
Stability

Inquisitive
Courage
Boldness
Curiosity

Liberal
Flexible
Enlightened
Inspirational

Ethical
Trustworthy
Virtuous
Noble

Eight Axioms of Honest Leadership, by David Watkins 2013

I assume that you notice some of the content within each axiom is personality driven and some behavioural. Therefore, some of these things you already "practice" – you are already doing them with your followers and it will be second nature to you. For example, in my view being "transparent" means that you behave in an open, communicative and tolerant manner. If this is the case you need not worry. Just carry on.

Equally, some of these things you just "are". Being "ethical" means you lead with a trustworthy, virtuous and noble style, or being inquisitive means you are courageous, bold and curious.

The axioms work as an integrated set. They work as one constant loop similar to a revolving wheel. And, as with any wheel, it has to have a hub, and in this case our hub is honest leadership. The axioms are complimentary and balanced – get a puncture in one area and you can help fix it with work on another. For example, get caught telling lies with suspicious sales techniques and you could neutralise any harmful consequences by introducing an ethical code of conduct.

Similarly, if your organisation is going through upheaval and change that removes a feeling of reliability and stability amongst your workforce, then the negative impact of this can be offset by a consistent and transparent communication policy.

The point is that whatever your personal situation, each of these axioms and their sub content needs to be placed by you into your own personal context and perspective of leadership. I am sure you have your own experiences and can tell your own stories behind each of the axioms. And you certainly will have your own opinion about the relevance of each when it comes to pursuing your own honest leadership approach. No-one can decide this for you.

Therefore *do not* look at these axioms as a top down or right to left list of tasks to plan and do. The use of the acronym "fidelity" is merely a method to help automatic recall of the axioms and help you implant the key aspects into memory. Important is that you learn to use your skill, personality and behaviour to move around the axioms depending on the scenario and context being faced.

Therefore, we must understand how we *anchor* these axioms into our sub-conscious and our daily activity, in order that all or some can become habit. Our aim should be to achieve "habitual honesty" in our leadership.

ANCHORING THE AXIOMS

Honest leadership is not just a matter of being truthful. Rather, it encompasses all the elements integrated within the eight axioms and combines these with concrete observable actions. This could mean that your honest leadership includes openly admitting to mistakes and failures, or not claiming credit for the accomplishments of others, or even keeping your promises or explaining why they can't be kept.

The axioms are not "one off" items where you create a fancy communication piece and call it a day. It is also not possible to make a "to-do" list of things that you have achieved, finalising each with a tick in the box once you have completed it. Anchoring these axioms is an on-going process of behavioural and in some cases intellectual or attitudinal change. Honesty is a never ending job; you have to maintain your focus to do these things and continually question yourself and monitor your actions.

> "Honesty is a never ending job; you have to maintain your focus to do these things and continually question yourself and monitor your actions"

But do not despair! Engendering honesty is in fact a competency that can be learned, applied and understood. It is something that you can get good at. As we have discovered, it is something that you can measure and improve, and something for which you can "move the needle". You cannot be an effective leader without trust and honesty. And following the guidance of the eight axioms will put you on the right path.

In this respect I provide a few ideas for your consideration, these being termed as "anchors". And like any anchor that sinks to the bottom of the sea, these ideas are intended to weigh down in your sub conscious and ensure that the axioms take root.

Of course these "anchors" can be mixed and matched as you deem appropriate. And clearly this list is not exhaustive – you need to stamp out your own hallmark on your journey and therefore use these anchoring ideas as inspiration and a kick start.

ANCHOR 1: LOOK IN THE MIRROR

The process of embedding honesty begins and ends with you. Even though this anchor covers the "Y" in fidelity, which at first glance may be seen as the last letter in our circle and acronym, remember that the journey to honest leadership is not an A – Z process.

You have to start by being honest with yourself; then you will be seen as honest by others, who will trust you and follow you. This is about building integrity and demonstrating moral intelligence. This means that self-honesty starts with the recognition of what your main responsibilities are – to yourself, to your followers, to your organisation and to other stakeholders.

Personal honesty also means accepting the things you discover. If you suffer from self-delusion or bias that everything is not your fault, or if you cannot accurately and honestly assess a situation – for example, you lay the blame at the door of difficult customers, an unreasonable boss or soft market conditions – then you mislead yourself and your team, and you will make faulty decisions.

Sabina Spencer in her book "The heart of Leadership" argues that authentic power *"shines from the inside out"*. She suggests that leaders should work to identify seven keys to authentic power and in doing this they will be able to free up energy and focus on providing inspirational leadership. Voicing truth is the fifth of these keys. Spencer argues that those of you who can unlock this key will display specific characteristics such as integrity, authenticity, self-expressiveness and commitment and have a tendency to be quality listeners, more innovative and well attuned to the world around you.

If on the other hand you feel more emotionally inexpressive, guarded, full of self-doubt, and others have told you (or you are even well aware) that you have a tendency to be somewhat cynical, superficial and rather flippant, take a long look in the mirror. You have some work to do in Spencer's eyes.

When standing in front of a mirror and looking at ourselves, it is quite challenging to realise that we do not often and openly state our own truths and beliefs. We hold back and instead often say what others want us to say. It is quite probable that you are kidding yourself if you believe otherwise, for most of us are controlled by the fear of humiliation. If we deny it, then our ego steps in; lending us a veneer of invincibility and protection when "attacked" and driving us towards success in a material orientated world. We know what to do, say, how, when and even why in order that we can advance and be seen to doing things right.

But as we continue to stare at our reflection, we also know that we have deeper values and beliefs. We know we should not always be toeing the party line. Therefore one of the greatest challenges is to be able to look at yourself and recognise your weak spots and be willing to tell the truth, about yourself to yourself. It is easy to maintain the status quo, as this avoids the need to confront transformation – but the deeper you look the sooner you realise that it is not necessarily contentment that keeps you from doing things, but rather fear.

> *"Most of us are controlled by the fear of humiliation. If we deny it, then our ego steps in; lending us a veneer of invincibility and protection"*

That is, fear of making a change and taking the steps that are needed to voice the truth.

Voicing the truth about your decisions and directions is one of the toughest and most important steps you need to take with yourself. Some of the models I propose in the Honestometer will help support you identifying where to start this process and become more conscious of the impact of your daily decisions.

When we are honest with ourselves, we are less afraid to be honest with others. "The truth will set you free" is echoed through the ages – go ahead, remove your glasses of self-deception, stand in front of a mirror and soak in what you see. As Spencer states, *"authentic leadership comes from finding out who we are, forgiving ourselves for being who we are not, and loving ourselves in spite of it all".*

ANCHOR 2: INCREASE YOUR FOCUS

To improve honesty, you need to focus on it. This takes courage. Fearlessly seek feedback from your boss and/or peers on any negative impact that you may be having on others. Hear what they say, thank them and act on it.

In his book "The Noticer, Sometimes all a person needs is a little perspective" Andy Andrews provides some interesting insights into how to "*do the right things*". He argues that focus is one of the key steps to moving in the right direction, which from our perspective should be habitual honest leadership. Have you ever noticed how when you focus on something, that "something" increases?

For example, if you focus on the fact that your car is old and needs a few thousand euros worth of repairs, you get a bit depressed. Then when you think about this and focus on it, what happens? You start to think of other things that you had forgotten about and you need to repair – the crack in the bathtub, the lawnmower which has blunt blades and needs fixing before next summer, the kids broken bike and so on. See? Focus increases the thing you're focusing on. And if that focus is on the wrong things, then you will feel even worse!

So with this in mind, try to focus instead on the things you need to do to instigate the axioms. Think about just one thing. For example, if you're the type who does not like to have an open office door, think for a few minutes about the message that your closed door provides to your team. Which axiom might this fall under? Does it demonstrate openness and communicative readiness on your part for example? Not really. Does it demonstrate that you're ready to guide others and act as an inspirational leader? Probably not – how could it when you put up a barrier between yourself and your followers?

You may argue that you're courageous, bold and inquisitive for instance – but does your team see you as being any of these when you sit behind a closed door? How would they know? When do you get their buy-in for your vision? If you have a closed door, presumably you interact only in pre-scheduled team meetings. Therefore there is a chance that you miss out on the ad-hoc chats that tend to foster in an open environment and within which you can encourage candid, passionate conversation as ideas pop into your head. These small things count and make a big difference in building an environment of trust and honesty.

So why not open the door? Focus on that. Think about what it may be like to open it. And I do not mean to be able to shout orders out of this open door. I mean to allow people the comfort and flexibility to walk in and get access to you. Allow them the chance to chat about things that concern them. These chats may only take two minutes and need no formal appointment, but they are important for personal well-being.

Focus on how they may feel if they can see you every day, and what happens when you are not just the invisible boss. And as you focus on this, you will find that your focus on the other things you are not doing as represented by the other axioms will also increase. You will automatically begin your personal journey to honest leadership.

ANCHOR 3: WORRY ONLY WHEN IT'S WORTH IT

Andrews also recommends to only worry about things that are worth worrying about. Place all of this into perspective. As Andrews rather eloquently states *"you worry, because you're smart... the dumber folks among us do not worry too much. They ain't afraid of nothing"*. The point being is that smart people are likely to be more creative and because of this smart people, especially leaders, tend to waste their creative energies worrying about things that *might, could* or *will* happen. In contrast less smart people simply look at someone else and claim, *"Heck; I can do that too"* and not worry about what may or may not happen.

As a result there is a risk that smart leaders misuse their time and imagination and begin to journey into dishonesty and self-destruction, sowing one lie after another to avoid the *"might, could or will"*. So this part of your thinking has to be turned off. And one way of doing that is through logic, which if you are smart, will appeal to you. That means thinking not about the possibilities but the *odds* of things actually happening.

Authoritative research according to Andrews shows that almost 40% of the things we think about never occur. So why worry about them? Equally, a further 30% have anyway already happened and it seems pointless wasting energy thinking about things that have already happened. 12% is needless stuff about our own health, for example achy legs, do I have cancer? Or I have a headache, is it a tumor? 10% of the time is spent worrying about what others think. And we can't do anything about what others think. So that leaves 8% for legitimate concerns. These are the things that you can actually deal with. And these 8% should be consistently and systematically broken down.

One very simple approach to starting this process is to write your concerns – real ones you can control – down. Keep a piece of paper by your bed, so when you wake up at night with your brain racing away with worries, you can write them down instead of trying to remember them. And do not be afraid to write them down every day. It may seem banal, but when you look back at the list it will help you place these worries into context and identify if there is something that really needs action. Presumably 92% can be ignored.

ANCHOR 4: COMMUNICATE WITH INSPIRATION

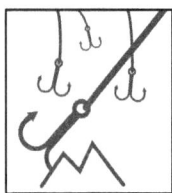

The challenge will grow as you experience success and witness cultural change and your followers' act and behave in ways you or your organisation has not experienced before. They may be more open. They may ask for things or comment on processes never before questioned. Employee engagement and other KPI may change. Employees may stay, others may go. And you must be ready and willing to accept this.

The key is to make sure that this change process remains healthy. Therefore it is critical to communicate. And I do not mean a quick town hall meeting and assume everyone is on board – the success of any communication lies within the receivers head; it is they who determine if they have understood what you are doing and saying. It is not for you to decide that your communication is successful just because you have done it. Therefore, create for yourself a simple golden rule: ensure every key change is communicated, communicated again and repeated some weeks later. Explain how, why, what and when. And use every channel available and then find some more.

Good communication will inspire. Great leaders engage through the heart, not through the head, and they are successful because they deal with emotions. Consider for example the rallying cry of Winston Churchill back in 1940: *"We shall go on to the end, we shall fight in France, we shall fight on the seas and oceans, we shall fight with growing confidence and growing strength in the air, we shall defend our Island, whatever the cost may be, we shall fight on the beaches, we shall fight on the landing grounds, we shall fight in the fields and in the streets, we shall fight in the hills, we shall never surrender"*. Today it seems to be rather full of pomp and circumstance, but he united the passion of a nation behind one cause. And 75 years later we still remember it.

> *"Good communication will inspire. Great leaders engage through the heart, not through the head and they are successful because they deal with emotions"*

But you do not have to be a politician to be a great communicator. Consider this one comment from Apple co-founder Steve Jobs *"Your time is limited, so don't waste it living someone else's life"*. Now consider what he achieved and what he will be remembered for, and it is soon clear that there are many emotions and thoughts that receivers could extract from these 12 words. In your quest for honesty and fulfilling these axioms, consider your communication approach. Here are some simple tips that you can work on when preparing your communication, be it direct, indirect or via third parties – and regardless of your chosen media.

Do not lie, or hide the truth: Eventually lies will catch you out. Tell it like it is. If it is bad news, say so, but tell people what you are doing to make it better. If it is good news, say so and thank people. Be humble. Be realistic, honest and hopeful. Integrity starts in your communication.

Be personal: Do not be afraid of sharing experiences and telling stories. If you stay at arm's length, then you can expect anyone you're communicating with to hold back and stay reserved. This will not promote a transparent and trusting culture and is not especially inspirational. Open up!

Avoid vagueness: Specificity is better than ambiguity. And this is true all the time. Therefore learn to communicate with clarity. Simple and concise is always better than complicated and confusing. Cut to the chase and hit the high points – tell people what you are going to say, then say it and tell them what you told them. Weed out the superfluous and make your words count.

Focus on giving: The best communicators are adept at transferring ideas, aligning expectations, inspiring actions and spreading their vision. Remember that communication is not for you – it's for your followers. Therefore focus on a clear communication that is well received and understood, and you will have accomplished your goal.

Have an open mind: Willingly seek out those who hold dissenting opinions and opposing positions with the goal of understanding what's on their mind, not convincing them to change position. This is always a big step, but having this background will help you re-align your communication to ensure that everyone has the chance to voice an opinion. This can help your approach provided you are liberal enough to accept different ideas.

Listen first: Great leaders know when to dial it up, dial it down and dial it off (mostly you should focus on down and off). This is not about top down monologue, but all around dialogue. Remove the earwax and stop talking. As Confucius once said *"we are given two ears and one mouth so we can listen twice as much as we speak".*

Be empathetic: Ensure that your communication is candid, empathetic and caring and not full of the prideful arrogance we may expect of an over inflated ego. Empathetic communicators display a level of authenticity and transparency that is not present with those who choose to communicate behind a carefully crafted facade. This approach will help you turn doubt into trust.

Be aware of your gaps: Be aware of what you are not saying or doing. What message does this give? Could someone read between the lines? Also do not outstay your welcome – be ready to clear the stage and let another replace you. Do not overload with rhetoric. Instead, keep your eyes and ears open and listen to the mood of the audience. Be ready to adapt and have a backup plan.

Know what you're talking about: Develop a technical command over your subject matter. If you don't possess subject matter expertise, few people will give you the time of day. Good communicators address both the "what" and "how" aspects of messaging so they don't fall prey to becoming the smooth talker who leaves people with the impression of form over substance.

Treat everyone as individuals, not as a mass: Work your communication to appeal to the individual. Choose words that appeal to one person and address them as one, rather than part of a large group. Establish credibility and trust at a personal level and the masses automatically follow.

The bottom line is that whenever you have something to communicate keep the content well-reasoned, specific, consistent, clear and accurate. Back it up with logic where needed. Spending a little extra time on the front end of the messaging curve will likely save you from considerable aggravation and brain damage on the back end. And most importantly of all, keep in mind that communication is not about you, your opinions, your positions or your circumstances. It is not for you – it is for your followers and listeners and adding value to their world. Do these things and you'll drastically reduce the number of problems you may otherwise experience moving forward on your journey to an honest leader.

ANCHOR 5: LOOK AROUND, BENCHMARK THE BEST

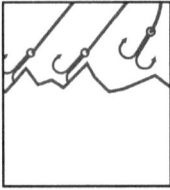

Benchmarking is also a great approach to supporting you on your journey to honest leadership. Do not be afraid to look over the fence – if you see a great idea there is no reason to be ashamed to borrow it and adapt it to your needs. Mark Twain said in "some national stupidities": *"The fact is the human race is not only slow about borrowing valuable ideas – it sometimes persists in not borrowing them at all"*. Now this is a book about honesty so I am not advocating plagiarism or stealing, but rather to consume an idea, reflect on it and instigate new creative approaches to make it your own.

It is often said *"If we don't know where we are going, we might end up somewhere else"* and *"those who benchmark do not have to reinvent the wheel"*. There is some truth to both statements. It is important to realise that benchmarking is not copying as it requires you to adapt what you have learned to your own needs and contextual setting. It is about comparing performance or processes in different organisations, or for our purposes comparing the activities between different leaders and learning how to do things better.

The main purpose of benchmarking is to improve your approach and performance by identifying where changes can be made. It goes beyond comparison of pricing or the features of competitors' products or services and simple task based decisions. Rather, benchmarking considers not only the result, but also the process and the practices that enable an organisation or yourself to achieve superior performance.

To do this properly you need to be sure what it is that you want to review and identify why. Identify those practices that most impress and then begin the process of adaptation. Identify a useful piece of an idea and build on it to make new situations and contexts. Or look at the ideas from a different perspective, or shift the structure of the idea to assemble solutions in different ways. If in doubt, pay tribute to the original idea but use it to instigate new creativity. As Warren Buffet once said *"It's better to hang out with people better than you. Pick out associates whose behaviour is better than yours and you'll drift in that direction"*. Look out for your benchmarks wisely and follow them!

ANCHOR 6: TAKE THE INITIATIVE

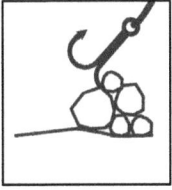

Consider this. There are five CEO's new to the idea of moral thinking. They all have a problem in their companies. Employees are leaving, customers are deserting, margins are down and things in general are looking pretty dire for each of them. One of the CEO's reads about the principles of Corporate Social Responsibility and decides that this is the big answer he has been searching for. How many CEO's are left who still have to implement CSR?

The answer is not four. It is still five. The point is, and it's worth repeating this, deciding is *not* the same as doing. It cannot be that we judge ourselves by our intentions and others by their actions. If all we do is intend, then we are no better than never doing anything in the first place. You have to *do*.

The job of a leader is to go first. But taking the initiative is tough. Who is first to tell the CEO bad news? Who is first to tell the employees that salaries are being frozen? Who is first to argue that launching a CSR campaign might enhance corporate reputation? The job of the leader in our context is to extend trust first. Not a blind trust without expectations and accountability, but rather a "smart trust" with clear expectations and strong accountability built into the process. People need to know what you expect, how they will be measured and the consequences of not meeting expectations. Conrad Hilton said "*Success seems to be connected with action. Successful people keep moving. They make mistakes, but they don't quit*".

But taking that first step is hard. Roosevelt's advice was to "do one thing every day that scares you". But in essence taking initiative is about seizing opportunities; it's about being proactive and not reactive. Mobilise and not hinder, cut through red tape and minimise bureaucracy. And take risks. That means you should stop reading and start acting. Identify what you are doing now, what you are not doing and would like to do, and determine the steps you can take to get where you want to go.

Anchor 7: Determine and support the span of control

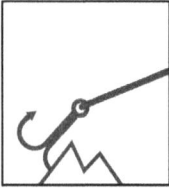

How many direct reports can you really handle? Five? Ten? More? The recent string of rogue trader cases, such as the £827 million loss at Barings Bank (that ultimately caused it to collapse) or the actions of Kweku Adoboli that cost UBS $2.3 billion demonstrate that company leaders cannot always know what is happening with their followers. Similarly, the scandal of telephone hijacking at Rupert Murdoch's News of the World was, he argued, unbeknown to him. Yet leaders are theoretically responsible for the actions of all their followers.

This is one of the dark aspects of leadership. You are forced to delegate authority and place trust in other people, but you do so with the risk that followers may let you down. They may fail to carry out essential tasks so that the rest of the company is impacted and the overall strategy goes off the rails; they may engage in power struggles with other subordinates in order to achieve personal advantage; they may even engage in fraud or other forms of criminal behaviour as the examples above show.

It is almost impossible to prevent that from happening. Certainly you must recognise that the problem exists. But you must also understand how far your influence can reach and lead accordingly.

This introduces the notion of span of control. It was first introduced by a British general, Sir Ian Hamilton, in a book entitled "The Soul and Body of an Army", published shortly after the First World War. General Hamilton concluded that most leaders have no idea of how to exert authority over large groups of people. Apart from problems of communication, most of us are not able to manage continuous on-going relationships with more than a handful of people at any one time.

Even in today's modern world the consensus is that you cannot cope with many more than 15 – 20 "relationships" and provide sufficient time for emotional contact to understand how your colleagues tick. Most of the time is spent virtually – how can you know what they think, how they behave and react to your decisions? How, for example, do people using social media sites such as Facebook have 300 so called friends? It is simply not possible to give each enough time to be able to class them as friends. At best they are acquaintances who are kept up to date as a result of you posting or tweeting your ideas and activities.

The most important aspect of leadership is the relationship you have with people – it is not just a matter of giving an order and getting it followed. We already know that people will behave and respond depending on how you treat them. For example, if you are a leader who is respected by others, and if you demonstrate to other people that you are trustworthy, there is a greater likelihood that other people around you will behave in a trustworthy manner too. Not a certainty; but a greater likelihood.

It is simply not possible for a leader to post and tweet ideas of honest leadership and corporate visions online. It is vital that your span of control, those people with whom you surround yourself day in and day out, is determined and they are trusted to help you cascade the messages to people within their span of control and so on down through the follower hierarchies.

And you can also support this process. Jack Welch, the former chairman of GE, spent much of his working life on the road, and often with new recruits. His purpose was not to make friends or indoctrinate employees to his way of thinking. Rather, it was to let them get to know him; to understand what he stood for, what his personal values were, what his expectations of them were. By the end of these visits and training sessions, Welch might not know his employees, but they certainly knew him.

Think about this as you embark on your own journey – who will be in your span of control? Why? How can they help you? When, why and how will you communicate with them and what will they do with their reports in their span of control. And get out of your office. Go on walkabout. Greet the people, do not tweet them or speak only through company newsletters. Be seen, felt, smelt and heard.

ANCHOR 8: SHOW YOU CARE

This is vital as 99% of the time you have to execute with people, not processes. This means you must show the people that you care about them and build a baseline trust. And people will determine the success or failure of your efforts. As Craig Weatherup, former CEO of PepsiCo said: *"When things are really tough, when it's unclear, when nobody knows what's really happening, they follow you because they think and because you've demonstrated that you really care about them... from the janitor to the chief of staff, affirm that person's human dignity. That's the one thing that inspires passionate followship"*.

This also means that you must walk the talk, which is challenging. Some of us believe that if we do the wrong thing and then come clean about it, that our ability to lead is lost. But in fact the contrary is true – the more sincere you are about your mistakes and then make a visible effort to fix them; the more likely you are to generate trust and respect. You only lose your authority in the eyes of followers when insufficient effort is made to right any wrongs.

Many of us can spot insincerity a mile away – there is something in the tone, in the body language or even as simple as the timing of an insincere apology that makes us question the validity of any apology. Key is to accept that on this journey to honest leadership you may make mistakes – but come clean about them. As Richard Branson said *"A company is people... employees want to know... am I being listened to or am I a cog in the wheel? People really need to feel wanted"*.

There are some simple rules that you can follow, such as:

- Act the same with yourself as you do when in public.
- Treat others as you would be treated.
- Do things from the heart; do not seek a reward for doing and helping.
- Mean and believe what you say; live it, demonstrate it.
- Use positive affirmations, but do not over praise; say thanks and mean it, but do not oversell it, the credibility is lost.

Anchor 9: Channel your time and energy

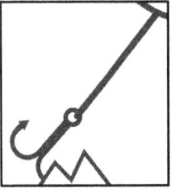

All of the ideas we have been talking about, all of the self-evident truths that we are referring to and all of the anchors we have covered need time. They need your focus and your energy.

The remarkable thing is that if you build a reputation for honesty these axioms become a self-fulfilling prophecy. But as with anything, when you want to have a payback, quantitative or qualitative, you have to invest your time, energy and maybe even a bit of resource. Invest this wisely and do so with focus, without unnecessary worry, with solid open communication and with comparisons to the best in class and you are onto a winner. Just make sure you continue to measure and challenge yourself – continue to look into the mirror and ensure the desire and passion to be honest remains within.

The mistake most of us make is that we assume that personal change takes time – but actually it does not have to. The time killer is *deciding* whether, what, why and how to change. The change itself is immediate. You can change instantaneously how you do business, how you treat your family and how you treat the people whose working lives have been entrusted to you. You can change the way you communicate and treat them and respect them. Change happens in a heartbeat once you have decided to change.

You can also change the credibility and the reputation you have by changing your approach, attitude and thinking towards honest leadership. But you must understand that there may be a lag between your deciding to change, making that change and for your reputation to catch up. Most of the people you deal with will try to work out, based on new evidence you present to them, what their new opinions are and that takes time. But sooner or later, as long as you are consistent, other people will change their feelings and opinions too.

Andrews stated: "*You can do whatever you want to do. You can accomplish whatever you want to accomplish. You are never lacking funds. The calendar is not your enemy. When you need to accomplish something great in your life you are only lacking an idea – time and money is [therefore] only a matter of perspective*".

Your own Honestometer

The journey is going well. Your dog is nearly home and you have decided to focus on some of the axioms and change your focus. You want to become a top dog, an honest leader. But this is a big step and some of you, I imagine, need a little more support. You need something to grasp onto, as we only have touchy feely stuff that can be a little slippery and hard to just "do". How do you check progress that you are on target? What measurable guidance and processes could be followed and used to help embed the Eight Axioms and the anchors into our daily activities?

For those of you who need some support, you are invited to create your own personal "Honestometer". To do this I provide a collection of templates that once you have seen them, you may decide can help you to stay on course or even identify what the course actually is along with the necessary stakeholders in the first place.

Some of these templates may be useful, others not. I also recommend that you refer to Mikael Korgerus and Roman Tschäpler's "decision book", a painstaking collection of 50 models that will guide you through some of the decisions that will face you on your journey.

Build your own collection (or adapt these) to your needs and in doing so, create your own personal "Honestometer". But do not just create one for the sake of being creative – you need to use it! And do so regularly as you embark on your journey, even if only for a sanity check and reminder of your actions. Good luck!

The Uffe Elb/AEK Model: The starting point of honesty is you. That means you also need to know yourself well. You need an "inside out" perspective of your strengths, weaknesses, beliefs, values and so on in order to understand how you mentally need to tackle the journey of honest leadership. You can use this model to get a general understanding of yourself and if needed, the same from others around you. It is in essence a public opinion model helping you understand your own personal traits and behaviours and a great place to start identifying the focus points on your journey to honest leadership.

The starting point is the diagram similar to the below, but you decide on the parameters you wish to use on the axis. Then, without giving a deep thought, rank yourself against the axis using for example a 1 – 10 scale – do you find it easy to lie, or do you struggle with yourself?

Do you have strong moral values or do you believe the end justifies the means? Do you lie or prefer to hide the truth? And so on until each line is ranked. Join the lines and create for yourself a spider diagram. Then ask your colleagues to do the same for you against each axis and compare results.

Of course this is only a snapshot view and nor is it especially scientific. But it will give you an initial gut reaction of where you fit and the things you should be considering as you start your journey to honest leadership.

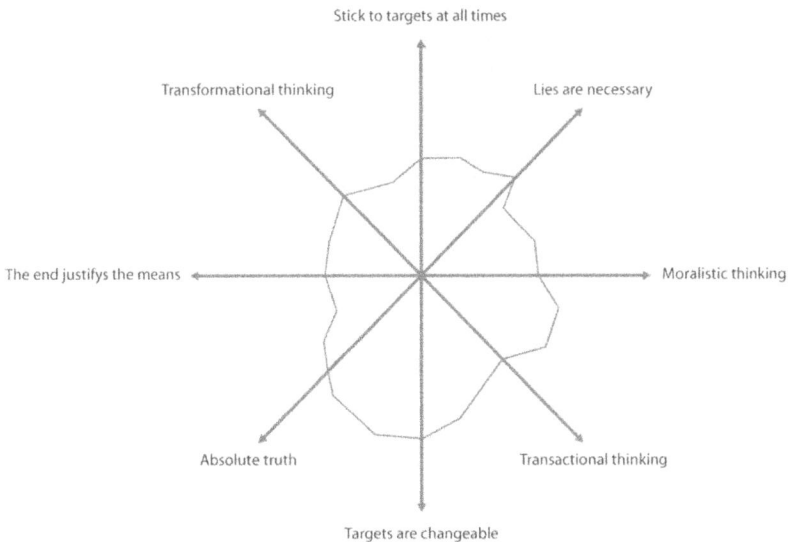

Inspired by the Uffe Elb/AEK Model

The seesaw/scales model: Another easy starting point is the seesaw or scales model. This however, is less about you and more about identifying the external factors that push or pull you towards honest leadership – it's a form of "outside in" thinking. Combined with the "inside out" information from the above model, the pair could contribute a powerful kick off in your planning.

A seesaw has to balance if it is to avoid falling to one side. Traditionally these models are used to illustrate for example Customer Perceived Value (CPV).

But this time around, rather than balancing costs and benefits, let's try a different perspective. What's wrong with developing a Perceived Value of Honest Leadership (PVHL)? On the one side identify all the things that are holding you back from being a more honest leader such as time, money, fear of failure, employee interest, other colleagues and so on. This could also include the perceived costs of embarking on a more honest approach.

On the other side pile up all the things that's urging you ahead, such as talent retention, need for CSR, open leadership, employee engagement. And include some benefits, ideally KPI targets too. You may even choose to rank and weigh the items in the list, giving each a percentage scale for example. Narrow the list down until you find a balance that suits you. The PVHL you are left with will identify the items you could be initiating; taking into account the challenges you face to start them in the first place.

Perceived pull and costs against honesty		Perceived push and benefit for honesty
Risk of failure, corporate culture		Corporate reputation
Employee suspicion/interest		Earnings per share
Stakeholders Influence/sustainability	Percived value of honest leadership	Employee engagement
Impact on bottom line		Talent Retention
Time & resource		

Inspired by Kotler's Customer Perceived Value (CPV) model

Stakeholder analysis: Before any journey has begun, you need to ensure who you are taking the journey with – you must identify your core stakeholders who have an interest in you doing what you are about to do. They may either be a help or a hindrance, but they need to be involved.

A stakeholder analysis is a useful process to undertake to capture these potentially interested parties. The first step is to simply list all parties who may be concerned with your activities. Stakeholders can be found in many of the following groups depending on the type of organisation. Direct stakeholders are those who are impacted by the decisions and actions you take. Indirect stakeholders are those who may have some influence or have an interest in the outcomes. Stakeholders may be:

- Shareholders
- Trustees
- Guarantors
- Investors
- Funding bodies
- Distribution partners
- Marketing partners
- Licensors
- Licensees
- Approving bodies
- Regulatory authorities
- Endorsers and 'recommenders'
- Advisors and consultants
- Employees
- Customers
- Suppliers
- The local, regional and national population (community)
- International communities
- Humankind (society, thinking sustainability, Corporate Social Responsibility)

It may seem superfluous to include many of the above – but remember, just because the connection is not yet clear, does not mean that they do not exist or the connection will exist in the future once you start on your journey to honest leadership. So it is best to include them early on.

Given that so many stakeholders are involved, it makes logical sense to ensure that their interests and needs are integrated and understand from the outset. Once you have the list of stakeholders, it is a good idea to understand how much effort is needed in meeting their expectations. This may depend upon the level of interest they hold and the power they have to influence the outcome of your journey.

One way of assessing this is to use an interest/power grid such as below. Plotting your stakeholders into this will help identify how "active or passive" you need to be: for example, a code of conduct can be a simple set of passive rules that are occasionally checked for adherence; but creating accountability may mean that you have to be more actively integrated. A more active honest approach is recommended for stakeholders representing higher power and interest in your activities.

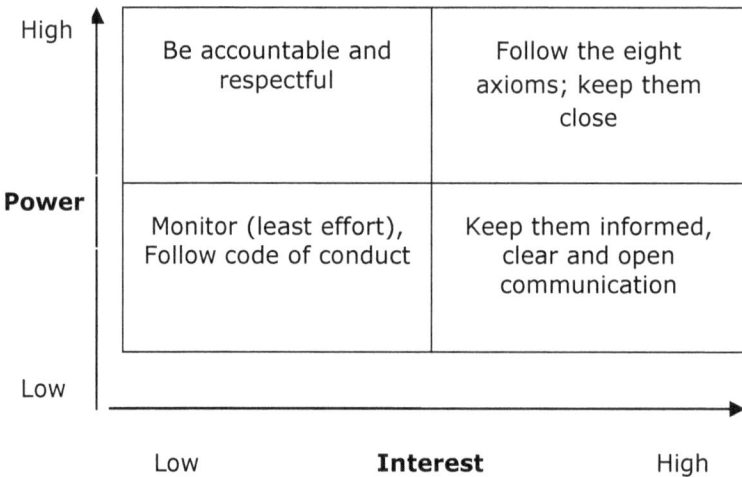

	Low Interest	High Interest
High Power	Be accountable and respectful	Follow the eight axioms; keep them close
Low Power	Monitor (least effort), Follow code of conduct	Keep them informed, clear and open communication

Inspired by the Stakeholder Analysis power/interest model by Eden and Ackermann 1998

For those stakeholders in the top two squares, especially the top right corner, you should also be asking yourself some basic questions to guide your actions and interaction with them. These questions may or may not include:

- What makes them stakeholders?
- Why do they hold the power / interest that they do?
- How and why must I interact with them? How often?
- What methods should I use to communicate?
- What issues may they have with honesty? Why is it important to them?
- How much can they contribute to or hinder my efforts? Why would they do this?

Some of these questions may not be easy to answer. One approach to lend additional clarity is to develop some kind of simplified "ranking" to help you understand the varying significance of the stakeholder relationships; the degree of impact or dependence between one another and your work.

This is not a precise science, but again, the difficulty in measuring the impact is no excuse for denying the existence of the relationship or possible relationship. The example below is only a suggested basic template. It attempts to ensure you understand who your stakeholders are, how they relate to you, what they need, the kind of KPI they may impact (all of these can be as specific as you wish) and most especially proposes a 1 – 4 scale for ranking their potential value and importance to you. The ranking is of course adaptable, but is intended to suggest the level of impact the stakeholder may have on

- Your financial performance (return to stockholders)
- Your corporate and/or leadership reputation
- Employee engagement
- Customer Loyalty

The table is a simple example of how this may be completed.

Stake-holder	Relation-ship to me	Their expectations	KPI impacted	Ranking
Investors	Creditor	ROI + EPS	Financial	4
Endorser, non exec. CEO	Sits on advisory board	Representation fees Stock options	Indirectly All	2 / 3
Regulatory body	Determines emissions rules	Alignment	Environ-mental R&D, Cost of production	3 / 4
Followers & online social site	Fan of my product	Opinion shaper for activities	None	1

Possible Ranking scale:

1 = Outside interest only. No measurable impact on financial KPI and corporate reputation. No influence on customers and employees.

2 = Limited interest. Perhaps with some coincidence may have a small influence on reputation, but cannot impact financial performance. The stakeholder may influence the opinion of a small number of employees and customers in the short term.

3 = Medium interest. Their influence could sway financial data and corporate reputation in the short term, but without any long term impact. May deter or attract employees and customers.

4 = High interest. The stakeholder will directly impact financial performance and corporate reputation, both in the short and long term. Has high impact on employee and customer satisfaction.

Undertaking a stakeholder analysis like this will help you to identify the full range of responsibilities that you and your organisation may have – and not just the obvious conventional requirements to produce a return on investment.

If you are in doubt as to stakeholder expectations and needs ask them what they are. Fundamentally this is all about understanding and respecting the needs of others, and as far as possible incorporating them into the philosophy, the aims, the processes and the activities of the organisation and meeting these with the right priority.

A final alternative that can help identify different interrelationships between you and your stakeholders is to sketch your "stakeholder family tree". This may help you identify which stakeholder is responsible for what and is another method to understand how much influence they may wield.

Start your family tree by putting yourself at the top. As in any family, place your "offspring" beneath you – but in this instance the offspring are the things you are most concerned about. In this example the same four factors are included as above: financial performance, corporate reputation, employee engagement and customer loyalty.

Placed under each of these "offspring" are the stakeholders, but they are listed in order of "birth" – in other words the order of perceived importance or influence to your offspring. For example, an investor is probably the most important stakeholder as far as your financial performance is concerned, and should be placed at the top of the tree under financial return.

Me/My Organization

Financial Return | Corporate Reputation | Employee Engagement | Customer Loyalty

Investors | PR | Leaders | Suppliers

Trustees | Marketing | Suppliers | Competitors

Regulations | | Marketing Partners |

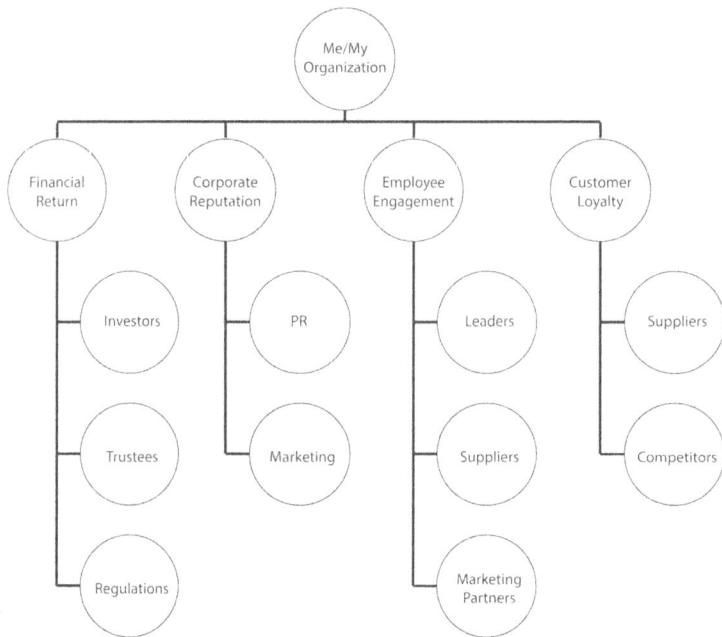

Finally, as with any family tree, children get married. So show the potential links that your stakeholders also have with one another. This simple exercise not only identifies which stakeholders are more influential to you for the things that matter, but also how they interrelate amongst themselves – boughs with more branches require more maintenance and you should also focus on these key indirect stakeholders.

The more you know and understand about your stakeholders, the easier your journey to honest leadership will be. Keeping the right partners informed at the right time, in the right way and for the right reasons makes sense. Consider this as a useful starting point for your Honestometer.

Root cause modelling: Some of the anchors recommend that you identify, record and focus on specific actions, problems and solutions. But to do this you first need to know what kind of problems you face, why they are there and then identify what you wish to do about them.

One common and simple method is to use root cause modeling, as often represented by the Ishikawa model, commonly known as "fish head or "herringbone" model. This was originally designed back in the 1960's as a quality control technique – and traditionally has been used to identify possible causes (for instance resource, people, processes, materials) and associated sub-causes to a manufacturing problem. It is in essence a mind map that forces you to take a step back and drill down into the challenges you face and identify their causes – which by implication should mean easier identification of resolution steps.

But there is no rule that stops you from using the same process to map out and get to grips with your honest leadership challenges. The example below demonstrates how we could use this, and in doing so helps to identify the "first steps" that you need to take to resolve these challenges. Key is that you stop wasting creative energies worrying about what might, could or will happen if you fail in your quest and rather channel these into problem solving and opportunity seeking. Try it!

How to use the tool:

STEP 1: IDENTIFY THE CHALLENGE

First, write down the exact challenge you face. Where appropriate, identify who is involved, what it is, when and where it occurs.

Then, write the core challenge in a box on the right (or left) side of a large sheet of paper, and draw a line across the paper horizontally from the box. This arrangement, looking like the head and spine of a fish, gives you space to develop ideas.

Example

Low employee
engagement

In this simple example, it is believed that employee engagement is an issue within the organisation.

Step 2: Work Out the Major Factors (causes) of the Challenge

Brainstorm, ideally with others, the factors that may be leading to this situation. Try to categorise them into broad headings, such as people, trust, climate, perceptions, systems, equipment, materials, external forces and so on. Try to draw out as many of these as possible. Each factor is drawn off of the spine, to create vertebrae:

Example

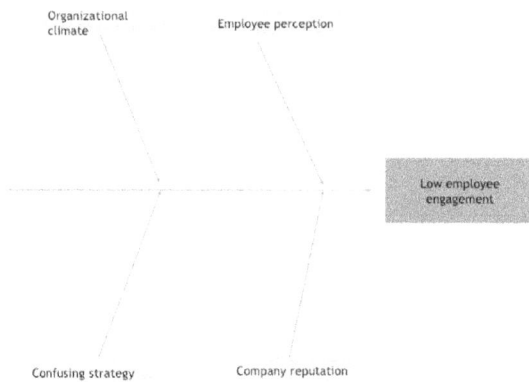

Now we have identified and mapped four potential drivers of the situation, in this instance:

- Organisational climate
- Employee perception
- Confusing strategy
- Company reputation

Step 3: Identify possible sub-causes

Now, for each of the factors you considered in step 2, repeat the exercise, drilling down into further possible sub-causes. Repeat this until no more causes can be identified.

Show these additional sub causes as further "bones" coming off of the vertebrae.

Example

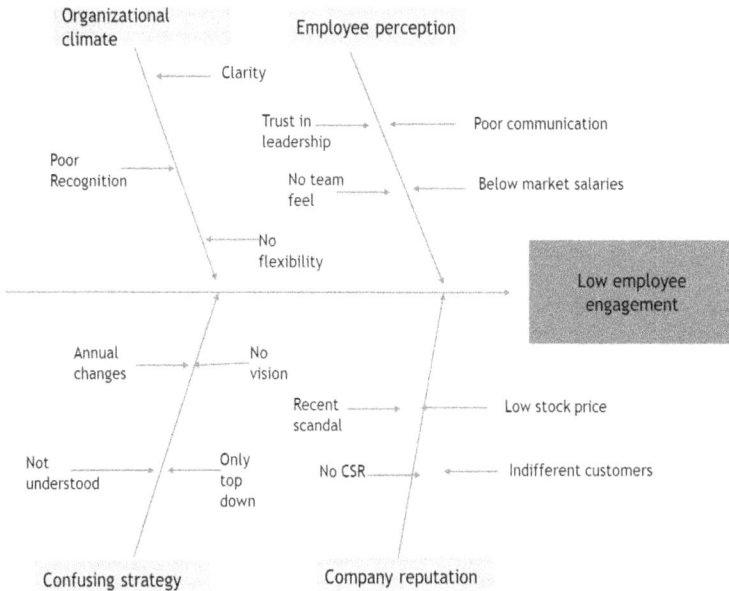

Step 4: Analyse Your Diagram

By this stage you should have a diagram showing all of the possible causes your initial the challenge.

You now need to decide what to do. This involves more work and quite probably other stakeholders, for which you could create a simple table such as the one below. Whether or not you decide to list all root causes and how detailed you choose to be with identifying their solutions, the associated responsibilities, the milestones and so on is a decision you can make.

I do however recommend ensuring that the progress on the resolutions is tracked. Many smart tools are available, such as MS Project that allow you to identify and track the inevitable detail as you progress. Google "Project Management software" for an idea of available web based applications. The list is exhaustive. But to start, this tool will help orientate your thoughts.

Cause	Solution	Who	€	KPI	Time
Confusing strategy					
Top down	Employee suggestion programme	Op. Board	€x	Ideas box	
Clarity	Communication	Comms.	€x	Quiz	
Employee Perception					
Trust	Leadership training	HR		Turnover	
Team commitment	Town hall meetings	HR/Line			
Below market salaries	Investigate, plan to adjust	HR		€ comparison	

The above template is pretty basic. But its value is that it forces you to drill down into the complexities of the challenges you face to identify potential solutions. It helps put mountains that may seem insurmountable into perspective. And in doing so makes it easier for you to use your anchors and work around the axioms.

The mapping exercise can minimise worry, enhance creative thinking, help improve your focus and allow you to better identify your benchmarking activities. It will not solve the battle, but at least will help with the identifying which soldiers you need, when, how and why. Therefore a valuable, simple and useful kick off tool.

Ethical competence scales: The journey to honest leadership is not only a case of understanding and internalising the characteristics and elements of honest leadership, but also must take the form of deep personal reflection. Some writers such as Dr. Desmond Berghofer in his book "Ethical Leadership Scales" espouse the use of three so called Ethical Scales to help this personal reflection process:

- Ethical Competence Scale
- Ethical Leadership Scale
- Ethical Organisation Scale

These help you analyse your personal progress and plot your personal record as well as engaging other leaders to help you. The scales are not too complex, but do need time to absorb and understand. Nevertheless I recommend that if you find value in their use, you should get hold of a copy and peruse them for more guidance.

In essence the three scales break down into 30 different "ethical competencies" and each of these competencies into further descriptive items. In total 80 items are measured across the three scales.

Ethical Competency scale: This will give you the experience of reflecting in a comprehensive and rigorous way on the level of your ethical competence across 30 items covering *personal ethical competence, social ethical competence and global ethical competence.* For example:

- Foundational characteristics: How we are grounded in thought and action.

- Empathy: How we strive to understand and appreciate the worth of others.
- Social skills: How we act to induce desirable, ethically grounded responses in others.
- Connections: How we act as part of a complex interconnected whole.
- Future orientation: How we act as responsible participants in creating a mutually beneficial future.

Ethical Leadership scale: This will engage you in reflecting more specifically on the leadership qualities needed to ensure your group or team maintains positive ethical relationships in all its work. There are 40 items on this scale, such as:

- Relationship to self: Personal qualities of the ethical leader.
- Relationship to others: Qualities that allow the ethical leader to connect with and empower others.
- Relationship to the whole: Qualities that reveal the ethical leaders sense of connection with a grand design and higher purpose.

Ethical organisation scale: This is used to check how well the organisation as a whole is doing across 10 issues such as:

- Economic considerations
- Relationships with the workforce
- Relationships with contractors and suppliers

You rank each of these items on a simple 1 – 10 scaling:

- 1 – 2: Never in place
- 3 – 4: Rarely in place
- 5 – 6: Sometimes in place
- 7 – 8: Usually in place
- 9 – 10: Always in place

The use of a 1 – 10 scale allows for the analysis of results in percentages, which of course even the least smart guys can grasp. For the record the end result is known as the Ethical Quotient (EthQ).

An example of one of the forms, in this instance for the competence "trustworthiness", which is an item in the ethical competence scale is shown below:

	How we are grounded in thought and action	Always in place	Usually in place	Some-times in place	Rarely in place	Never in place	Alloca-ted value
Characte-ristic	Explanation	10 – 9	8 – 7	6 – 5	4 – 3	2 – 1	
	Being reliable and dependable						
	Being willing to admit mistakes						
	Being true to your word						
	Being worthy of confidence						
	Keeping promises						

Taken from the Ethical Quotient model by Dr Desmond Berghofer

No claim can be made as to the accuracy of such a system – for a start it is judgmental. But it is thorough, and will enable you to analyse in some detail where work remains to be done. You need to be prepared for and accept the results.

Not one of these templates that you may wish to include into your Honestometer can claim to be accurate, scientific and valuable. This has to be a judgment call only you can make. On the other side, if you are serious about becoming an honest leader, and you decide to monitor your progress (which you ought to do) the measurement process should be open and honest too.

Our first anchor suggested to "look into the mirror" and argued that honesty starts – and ends – with you. If you cannot ask the right questions of yourself to complete these templates, or shy away from building your own Honestometer, or kid yourself about the results, or find excuses to explain the results rather than trying to understand them, it can only be concluded that you have a long journey ahead, and quite probably you will never reach your destination.

Your path to the Eight Axioms of Honest Leadership starts now. You have the background. You understand what honesty is (and isn't), you understand the role of a leader. You know that being honest pays off and you have the tools to start. What are you waiting for?

PART V
SEARCHING THE TRUTH
OF OTHERS

At the start of this book I promised a thought provoking read. I hope I have achieved that. But it is not only about what I think; I believe we should also consider the perspective of others; and this is what this Part is all about.

I follow with the input of other leaders who have kindly taken the time to put finger to keyboard and knock out a few words about honesty and honest leadership.

Getting this input is not about adding "glitz and glamour" – only about getting a different perspective on a hot topic. The contributions should enable you to consider your stance with different eyes and ears; some of them may ring true to your own experience, values and opinions. I hope and dare to presume that they continue to provoke thought and help you along your personal journey.

Each article is summarised with the name of the author, and follows in alphabetical order. I have allowed myself in some cases to make editorial fine-tuning; the changes are approved by the contributors and represent their efforts.

HONESTY IN LEADERSHIP

By David Barker, Managing Director, The Learning Eye

An interesting word, "honesty": In my view it is a much abused and often miss used word. Is it ever possible to be absolutely honest in either personal or business life? Really?

Simple white lies about the quality of a child's drawing or the new colour of a partner's hair are all part of a tissue of 'bended truths' that we all use to survive in the world and not hurt other's feelings. Absolute honesty is therefore only real as a childlike state in which we are excused indiscrete observations due to age and inexperience. It exists only until the child has learnt that 'absolute honesty' is not an acceptable state in which to travel through life!

Honesty is therefore a relative term which we have to learn to internally define for ourselves and as such varies according to our own moral and personal standards. However these standards often include the social values of the society in which we live. We know if we go against these, the rule of law will ensure we will be punished.

My own personal view is that honesty is about being true to your own set of social and moral values, regardless of what is happening around you. If you kid yourself, then what does that say about you?

Allow me to illustrate with two personal examples. The first comes from an experience in dealing with my customers, with whom I had built a close relationship and considered my peers.

They were valuable customers of a company I had founded and had decided to sell after 13 years. Part of the agreement enabled me to take these customers with me.

At the time of leaving the customers were not aware of my decision, and nor had I finalised all the details of my next steps – as a consequence it was agreed that I could continue to "trade" under my old company name, within the legal bounds of course, and maintain their custom. Of course, loyal customers appreciate stability and a change of ownership sometimes jeopardises good business. It was suggested that the customers would not even be aware of this shift.

For me however, it just didn't "feel" right not to inform them. Therefore I decided to advise the customer of the situation, warts and all, placing at risk my relationship with them, business for my old company and of course, my reputation. It was unlikely they would find out but if they did it could have caused huge trust problems and cancellations of various projects.

As it happened, the honest approach was well received and they remained loyal, forming a cornerstone of my new business which was then successfully floated on the stock market in London two years later. I was later told that our relationship was quoted as key to the float, which for me is a positive and unforeseen consequence of honesty.

The second example came during the immediate aftermath of the 9/11 crisis. In my industry at the time we started receiving almost immediate signals of delayed or cancelled projects, supported by all means of excuses such as fear, economic uncertainty, banned travel, budget cuts and so on. In essence we estimated that we would see business nose dive by some 30% – we needed to reduce our staff costs quickly.

I decided to take legal advice and was told we could cite the significant change in the business environment and could start reducing our head count quickly. However, this once again clashed with my personal values – how can it be that I cut the very people who had helped grow my organisation, without giving them options or discussing it first. Morally, it seemed I owed them some kind of "chance" in this sticky situation.

Therefore we held an open meeting, and proposed that everyone take a pay cut for a period of time rather than experience redundancies. Of course the risk being that if one dissented, the plan would derail. But after an honest, open meeting, common agreement was taken to reduce salaries by 30%, thereby saving the business, gaining respect for all, and building a fantastic environment of camaraderie and commitment.

In an age where our MP's get accused of rebuilding their homes using expenses, church leaders for child abuse and sports heroes for narcotics use, what hope do we have to find honest leadership? I believe honest leadership starts with us and ends with us. It is up to us to follow what we believe is right, and not follow the crowd. If we argue things will never change, yet make no effort to change ourselves, are we any better?

HONESTY IN POLITICS: CRAFTING THE BALANCE BETWEEN POPULISM, POPULARITY AND PERSONALITY

By Trix Heberlein, former president of the National Council of Switzerland (1998/99)

I would like to discuss the subject of honesty from the perspective of politics; I can imagine that some of you are now sitting up and taking note. After all, and perhaps we can be blunt here – the world of politics may not be the first place many of us would think of when investigating the idea of honesty and honest leadership.

But considering my experience, I believe I am well placed to share my perspectives that reflect the challenges of leading an honest political life. Entering politics is quite an experience. "First timers" have to start with a campaign, meaning you have to "sell" yourself and your qualities and in doing so explain to everyone who knows you and many that don't, why you are running for a political office – and more to the point why they should back and support your efforts.

In the Swiss parliamentary electoral system you begin by getting your name onto a list of candidates proposed by a Party. You are thus competing with colleagues of that same Party. The first attempt at this will in all likelihood be unsuccessful; but the second time around you may succeed and find that you enter a parliament or a local executive with the responsibilities of the voters resting on your shoulders.

And this is your first moment of complete self-awareness! Suddenly all your words, actions, thoughts and beliefs come to the forefront: what do they, your voters, expect from you, why did they want you to represent them in this function? Do they expect you to lead? If so what? And are you an example of what you stand for? Do you really "walk the talk"?

For me, it was always clear – I had been elected not only because of the party I represented, but also a large part due to my past achievements and political positioning. As a family mother, lawyer and a liberal I always tried to ensure my public life followed the principles I strongly advocated. Even though I was not a full time lawyer whilst raising my family, I was heavily integrated with different foundations, NGO's or offices of our local community where we lived. I was (am) especially passionate about people motivation and encourage females to seek political mandates and responsibilities. Therefore, once I was asked to do the same, I could not really refuse to participate when I was asked to be a candidate for the cantonal (regional) parliament.

But once elected, you begin to ask a lot of personal questions: what does it mean for you; what does it mean for the people who have chosen you as your representative, and clearly what does it mean for the people around you and for your family? And this is the tough part – being a politician, you have to accept that you are in the public eye, meaning you may invite criticism as much as praise and you are closely followed by the media.

And this means that a politician has to consistently find a balance between their values and personality and the voters' expectations of being both a populist and popular. They need to like and respect you and also understand and accept what you stand for. Therefore, transparency must be an essential basis of honest politicians and your family has to be prepared for this. They must also take care of their activities. This does not mean that you have no privacy, but that the members of your family also become public in the eyes of the media. And whilst it is possible to define certain limits, it is not especially pleasant to live with the risk of finding a family story hung out to dry in the local media!

Fortunately when these limits are respected, they can also add to the credibility of a politician. For me achieving family transparency and credibility was more important than superficial popularity or populism. Resisting the temptation of quick wins and gaining short term publicity, especially before and during election periods, is no easy task. Today the media is very demanding and expect you to take a position, publish an opinion or become active in the different platforms that abound, such as Twitter, online blogs or Facebook – and often before you have had the time to seriously think about an issue.

Absolute transparency is a critical success factor in winning the hearts and minds of your voters and gaining personal credibility. This may concern what you represent in politics and why you take this position, or why you have made a specific decision or support a particular viewpoint. This means, you also have to admit that you cannot be a specialist or be informed about all the various items parliament has to treat and discuss. Therefore you are also heavily dependent upon the different committees that are responsible for preparing the topics; in short you have to learn to trust the specialists of your Party's responsible persons.

This does not mean that you should not ask questions and express your opinion. To be ready to learn, to be open to listen to new arguments and to respect the opinion of your opponents are further essential attributes you need if you want to be accepted and successful in politics. It also means that being honest means to be true to yourself: to have a strong character and to stand for your convictions even when the wind blows in an opposite direction. This should not prevent you however from self-criticism and the willingness to listen to people's ideas and opinions – which is not always an easy task. But in my opinion this is an absolute necessity if you want to be credible and convincing.

In our (Swiss) political system of many parties and a coalition government consisting of at least four of these parties, we have to find majorities to be able to make progress. This means we must accept that there is not an absolute truth and that politics demand tolerance. We have to find solutions which can be accepted by a majority of the people and which help to preserve our country's position and stability. As a small country we have to compete with all the others in difficult economic and political times.

To lead a life that visibly and publicly demonstrates your convictions demands authenticity, even though in our (any) political system you can never achieve 100% perfect approval rating. But you have to be able to explain why this result is the best that can be achieved under the given circumstances.

Honesty in politics, in fact honesty for any political leader is not in my view any different than the honesty that one should expect from business leaders. Being politically active demands patience and sometimes a detour if you cannot reach the optimum – this does not mean that you should not defend your opinion, it is essential to remain yourself and to be credible in what you stand for. But business leaders as politicians must also demonstrate a willingness to change and be open for different perspectives. Children teach you every day that you cannot demand from them what you don't live yourself. This is no different in politics or in business.

Perhaps the idea of finding "honesty" in politics and politicians is at times rather questionable. It is admittedly not always lived in the purest form. Let me give you an example out of the elections for a federal counsel position (the Swiss executive government). The candidates for this body are drawn from the elected parties. There are always more candidates than members that can be elected, which clearly results in discussions, proposals or agreements within the parties who will jostle amongst themselves to nominate their preferred representatives.

After the elections the loosing candidates will be told the usual apologies and hear the confirmations of past and continued support. But in actual fact, if a "looser" was to count all the voices of support versus the actual votes received, the discrepancy is high. So someone somewhere is lying and when push came to shove, did not proffer the promised vote. But this dishonesty amongst colleagues is unfortunately "normal" not only in politics, but also in business.

To conclude, transparency and honesty in politics, regardless of the position you have, is essential for a "public person". Once you are elected, you become a person who must live, work and play in the public eye, acting as you have promised and representing their needs and values. Of course nobody is perfect, but self and social awareness become paramount as you conduct your daily lives as an individual and with your family and friends. You must live and breathe honesty; you must become its ambassador.

A MOMENT OF TRUTH

By Daniel Huber, Vice President Human Resources Switzerland Alstom Switzerland Ltd.

The meeting with the CEO had been fruitful and efficient, and would come to an end soon – or so I had thought. To my surprise the CEO stared at me and added: *"By the way, Daniel, you should not have told Frank about his termination. You should have given him an excuse. To tell him the truth was a mistake."*

Instead of justifying my behaviour, I just smiled and said: *"Even though you believe it was a mistake to tell the truth, John: I know that it was the right thing to do, and I would do it again."*

Every so often many business leaders will experience a watershed moment. And this conversation turned out to be one such moment for me. What had happened? A few months earlier I had inherited a delicate task: in my role as Head of Human Resources in a multinational company I had to invite a top manager, let's call him Frank, to a meeting at our global headquarters. This meeting was planned to terminate his contract.

Frank had quite a long flight to make for this meeting, and clearly looked for an understanding as to why it was necessary to hop onto a plane at rather short notice. I called him to explain that this was about an important business issue. However, the timing for such a meeting was somewhat illogical and Frank being a rather astute guy suddenly asked me *"Daniel, will you terminate my job?"*

And that was it. This was to be my critical moment of truth. I was faced with a clear and very direct question and had two seconds to take a decision: should I tell Frank a lie, although the answer to his question was a clear, direct "yes" – or should I be honest and tell him the brutal truth?

I believe that honesty is one of the pillars of human ethics. Real ethics never remains abstract or theoretical. Real ethics is always practical and directly linked to a specific situation in life. You do it or you do not. It comes from within. However, although practical, honesty is not a value in itself, particularly not in the context of leadership. Honesty is the indispensable basis of the most important driver of leadership and teamwork: trust.

Trust is an inherit part of leadership. Team members must have the comfort to trust that their leader is serving in everyone's best interest, and leaders have to trust their followers that they are fulfilling their responsibilities. Thus, it is imperative that leaders perform their leadership with honesty. Instead of "honesty" I could write "integrity" or "authenticity". In my view and in this context, they are equivalent.

In a business world with increasing complexity, globalisation and uncertainty, self-awareness is pivotal for leaders. Self-awareness requires a high level of honesty, of integrity, of authenticity. This counts for far more than the lectures contained within any management book. Indeed, 2400 years ago Plato described four Cardinal Virtues – today he might call them "core competencies": prudent, considerate, brave and fair.

In an attempt to combine my experience as a business leader with my studies in philosophy, I understand Plato's Cardinal Virtues as a set of very useful, reasonable considerations:

Prudent: a leader must be able to keep the balance between IQ and EQ, and master a high level of self-reflection. This combination leads to wisdom and acting in a prudent way.

Considerate: a leader must be able to listen carefully – and not make the sadly common mistake where they believe that great communication means talking a lot! Successful communication is dependent upon the receiver – not the sender. Listening carefully enables the leader to think things through and avoid what appears to be a "quick wins" but which all too often turn out to be hasty actions. Being considerate leads to sustainable decision taking.

Brave: a leader must have the courage to think out of the box, to take risks, be transformational thinkers and to build a vision and with this vision to inspire their team. Brave also means to be decisive, to take accountability, instead of looking for others to be blamed in the event of a poor decision.

Fair: a leader must be a role model and "walk the talk", treating others they themselves expect to be treated. To be a role model means to be lawful, balanced in their own actions, and treating team members with equal respect. Fairness is a key driver of motivation.

Having read many management books over the years, I dare to argue that the majority of the management literature is more or less a repetition or extrapolation of Plato's Cardinal Virtues, albeit packed in a more modern perspective.

Interestingly enough, you may note that the words "honesty", "integrity" and "authenticity" are not part of Plato's Cardinal Virtues. Perhaps he did not consider these aspects as important enough to be integrated? Saying that, I believe that honesty, integrity, authenticity forms the nucleus of Plato's considerations. For him, as one of the most influential philosophers of humankind, it was just not feasible to be prudent, considerate, brave or fair without being honest. Honest with one self, and honest with others that make up a community or society.

I have now shared my theoretical and practical beliefs: but allow me to conclude and close with my "moment of truth" with which I began my contribution.

After the meeting with the CEO and his remark that I should "hide the truth" I allowed myself some personal reflection time. After all, I had chosen a completely different tact than our CEO (and other members of the Board as I later discovered) would have done. They would have fed Frank the lie on the phone prior to his trip and dumped the truth during the face to face grilling.

You can imagine that I had followed my personal beliefs and intuition when confronted with that clear, direct and delicate question. The termination of Frank's contract is not the most pleasant of memories I retain, but it went reasonably smoothly and without the turbulences most parties had expected beforehand.

When the whole process was over, Frank wanted to see me before he left the company. *"You know, Daniel"* he told me *"I would have created a big mess for the company, including a nasty court case, if you had lied to me on the phone. But since you had been courageous enough to tell me truth, I knew that I could trust you, during the whole process, and that you would not lie to me or treat me as badly as some others in this company did. I could simply rely on you. Believe me: your courage to tell me the truth from the very beginning saved the company a lot of money and energy. I will remember this when being a leader in my next job."*

THE UNEXPECTED LINK BETWEEN PEOPLE LEADERS AND DOG TRAINERS

By Helene Leimer, B.A., interpreter, psychologist and author of "the thing with the dummy – 40 questions and answers on the way to a successful dog working test".

When I consider the aspects of "guiding, managing and leading" and apply these to the principles of people leadership, dog training and dog ownership, bizarre as it may seem, I believe that there are many parallels to be found. I think this is important to write about in view of the title of the book.

It is the nature of dogs that allows us to draw these remarkable parallels and get down to the surprising similarity between people leadership and dog training. Just like people, dogs like to be led in an open honest way. Give them this respect, and like us, they will give you the results that a leader (or a dog owner) is looking for. Let me explain my perspective.

When leading people in a global business environment we often refer to the tasks facing the "normal person". But what is a normal person? All people are different, and as humans we work hard to carve out our own identities based on our expectations, values and of course the input and guidance we receive from our leaders.

Nevertheless, we could argue that normal people are those who tend to follow societal expectations, acknowledge usual and "accepted" interpretations of right and wrong and appear to be happy to follow strong leadership. Of course there are always exceptions to the rule, but let us at least agree that most of us are "normal" law abiding citizens that do not aim to go through life doing a bad job or question and disrupt socially accepted principles.

But is this the same with dogs? We could argue that dogs, if allowed to live and breed following their natural devices will also create their own identity. And dog trainers like to refer to "normal" dogs just like business leaders like to refer to "normal" people. For many professional dog breeders and trainers, including myself, I believe a normal dog is one that is reared and kept according to its genetic background. More to the point, respect this background in the same manner a leader should respect the follower, and the results will be far more successful than not.

Many dogs can be trained to fulfill specific tasks and become experts at doing it. Show dogs are trained to do just that – show off and look good. Hunting dogs are bred and trained to hunt and retrieve. This is the same with people. Train them in a specific task, and often they will learn how to master it. But they will never internalise and optimise these tasks if their heart is not in it.

Rather the leader should lead with trust and passion. A leader who gives people the freedom and trust to follow their natural instinct will more often than not have a reasonably engaged workforce trying hard to do the right thing. And this is the same with dogs. Those that are *allowed* to follow their natural instinct will also lead a life displaying uncompromising and loyal honesty towards its owner.

I intentionally place the word "allowed" in the paragraph above in italics; most dog owners believe their dogs to be subordinate just like some business leaders may view their employees to be subordinate. And in thinking this, many dog owners proceed to educate and instruct their dog and expect an appropriate result or response in return.

This places the burden of "failure" automatically over to the dog if its behaviour is not what we expect it to be. Surely, if we as owners have told, taught and conditioned the dog again and again, it would have figured it out pretty quickly, right? The dog simply "has" to know! It should sit when told to sit. Lie down when told to lie down. This drill instructor regime is designed to condition the dog into absolute obedience. And the closest parallel we can find to this when we consider people leadership can be found in the armed forces. Regardless of external circumstances, mental state, headaches, backaches or other stress, military personnel are drilled into following orders.

The *top dog,* be they an army commander or dog owner in these examples, commands and expects the *underdog* to always promptly deliver that which has been methodically drummed into them. More often than not, the top dog believes these expectations to be justified and refuses to listen to reason; their superior attitude entitles them to occupy the moral high ground. Knowingly or unknowingly, people like control. In my view, self-awareness, critical questioning and personal are suppressed and emotion is often absent in this leadership & ownership style.

And a lack of emotion can create resentment amongst the followers –

whether human or dogs. Followers do not respond well in the long term to direct, authoritative and dishonest leadership. Followers will cease to follow and will leave. Similarly dogs will sniff out a new owner if we let them!

To avoid this, leaders, dog owners or trainers alike should channel their energies not for personal gain, power or maintenance of position; rather they should use their creativity to be frank, approachable, understanding and prepared for open communication. This approach to "guiding, managing and leading" consists of four pillars which not only form a fundamental basis for people leadership and honest team work, but also are vital for safe, secure and successful dog training:

Definition of short, middle and long term targets: These are combined with a stepped plan to achieve those targets.

Definition of participating personalities: Such as human versus dog; owner versus trainer; leader versus employee plus the creation of SMART goals to adapt to the speed and capabilities of these personalities.

Clear positioning: This is based on the findings in point 2 to allow for the gradual preparation of handling security. This step is essential because the dog needs the security of his master to perceive him as authentic and to accept his signals and commands without confusion. People are no different; followers need to be able to trust their leader and have clarity in communication to be able to maximise personal performance.

Ongoing quality control: The attitude of the (dog) trainer towards his protégé has to be permanently monitored and when needed corrected to ensure that the targets are achieved and when deviation is apparent, corrective measures are taken. It is vital that while doing this the leader / trainer has the necessary motivation and self-awareness to maintain positive teamwork with the "performer" (the retrieving dog) and ensure emotions on both sides remain positive, rather than frustrated or annoyed.

Of course, a clear advantage that a dog trainer has over a business leader is that the dog cannot lie; the dog will not say one thing and do another; it will not busily follow your guidance whilst working to undo your good work behind your back. It is not interested in its own power, rather only a master that it can trust and bond with. In this respect the leader can learn from the led.

However, both dog trainers and business leaders do share a common responsibility to lead honestly and engage their followers. The better they achieve this, the faster a trusting connection between the *top dog* and the *underdog* will develop. Honesty leads to trust, trust leads to loyalty, loyalty leads to reliability and in the end a permanent bond between the leaders and followers – regardless of whether they have two or four legs.

PART VI
THE SEARCH IS OVER

"Being a leader is hard; being an honest leader harder still."
– David Watkins

I wrote this book with the intention of investigating honesty. And in doing so, link this specifically to a passion of mine: "great leadership".

The fact that both of these subjects are frequently in the world headlines and often in combination with one another led me to believe that I was not the only one fascinated by these things. But what worries me however, is that many of these headlines tend to be negative when compared to the ideals of "honesty" and "great leadership" – which I believe shows that we are perhaps approaching a crisis point, from which there is no return. Without some care, we are at danger of entering a new phase where "dishonesty" becomes the new and accepted leadership "norm".

Some authors are arguing that we cannot get through our day without lying. This forces me to ask what hope for the future does mankind have? It may appear that even the Church has given up – after all, at the beginning of 2013 the Pope resigned and in doing so became the first in 600 years to take this radical step. He cited age and health reasons but left behind a series of nasty "vatileaks" including alleged jealousies, money laundering, sex scandals, stolen documents and other unpleasant deeds, all of which have allowed us to witness another side of the previously secret heart of the Catholic Church.

As a result of all this I decided to throw my own opinion onto the debating table. This is not intended to escalate the situation, but rather to educate and in doing so proffer a resolution. And not just any resolution that is driven only by non-achievable ideals – rather one that is easy to understand and recall and above all can be internalised and optimised by each and every one of us.

I believe that great leaders are those that command respect – and respect is earned through being honest in your dealings with both yourself and with others. Surely, it cannot be that we have to lie just to survive the day? Can it? Are we really ready to throw in the towel on our values just to generate profit? Do we really not care about the well-being of our friends, colleagues and followers? Somehow, I think at most of us do, and those of you who have followed this journey are I hope ready to make that first step, and look into the mirror.

At this point you have a choice. If you appreciate the candour and openness that surrounds a self-aware individual, and you strive for a reputation based on positive honest actions, then think deeply about the pages you have read. Do not try to lead others; simply express yourself openly and fully, and let others follow you. And they will. Lose your ego and a great team will be ready to come with you!

But don't kid yourself. It will not be an easy journey. There will be times when the temptation to tell a small fib or to hide some tiny truth, at someone else's expense, will surface. But do all you can to stay on course and remember it is not for nothing. We know that following a moral compass at least plays a part in achieving long term organisational benefits that combine with an image enhancement that you and / or your organisation can achieve.

We all know that when honesty and transparency are lacking there can be no trust and when trust levels break down there will be no loyalty and without loyalty we struggle to achieve our goals. It is impossible to cultivate a climate of trust in the absence of ethics, honesty and transparency. Consequently fairness, accountability and responsibility cannot and will not exist if we dismiss the idea of honest leadership.

With the aid of the Eight Axioms to Honest Leadership, my proposed anchors and the Honestometer, you now have the tools to start your personal journey that will, if you put your heart and mind to it, enable you to identify, train and maybe even tame your own leadership approach and help you to become a "top dog".

But do more than just "think about it". You must follow through as intention is not the same as *actually doing*. Become an ambassador of honesty and proudly wear its colours. For the more experienced amongst you, there are no excuses; an old dog can still learn new tricks.

SOME PRIVATE THOUGHTS YOU SHOULD KNOW

Over the years throughout my corporate career, I have heard varying comments from a succession of line managers:

"You are too fast for the organisation"

"You're too creative – please stick to the details"

"We are transactional – do not try to transform us!"

"Theory and idea has no place in our organisation – we stick to what we do best"

"You talk too much"

"You are too open and honest – better to keep your mouth shut"

"I always wonder what it is you are keeping from me" (I had at this stage been learning from the quote above)

"You're now over 40 – everyone should write a book before they die"

This last one came from my wife. Her grandfather had written many books about the political history of Southern Africa and in doing so had left behind a personal legacy she frequently refers to.

He had managed to record something down he believed in and had an opinion about. And in doing so he enabled others to learn and grow from his experience and opinion and also left behind a proud family, including many dogs, when he finally passed away.

In contrast, I had managed to churn out some University and MBA study papers, and achieved some great results that I and my professors were proud about. I even remember winning a "best thesis" award which is quite a nice thing to achieve. But no-one else really knows too much about my work. Therefore, as a seasoned professional in the learning & development world I decided I could do more than I have done to date to share my experiences and ideas.

Indeed, I spend my time talking, teaching and preaching to leaders about what they should be doing to become even better leaders. So, I decided, why should I not put some of these things onto paper and enable others to gain some additional insights?

And this is what you have just read. I have shared my ideas, opinions and feelings. The decision to take this step was easy, as was the title of the book. Dogs are honest. People are often not. People development, and by implication leaders and leadership, is important to me. It's what I do. And I am told I am good at it and should share more of it.

I decided to concentrate on "honesty". For me this is a trait/characteristic/value/moral [insert or delete as you wish] that is sadly lacking in our private, public and professional lives today.

I had started writing this book feeling somewhat frustrated at the world around me. I finished it grateful for the journey I have had and as a result clearer of the decisions that lie ahead. I also now own a dog.

Thanks for reading.

David B. Watkins. April 2013

PART VII
FURTHER SEARCHING

If I have extracted an article or quotes from a book via the web, the address is also included.

BOOKS USED AND THAT I RECOMMEND

Akerlof, G: Loyalty Filters American Economic Review 73 54-63(page 61)

"Anderson, E: If God is dead, is everything permitted." In Hitchens, Christopher (2007). *The Portable Atheist: Essential Readings for the Nonbeliever, Chapter 5. Also accessible over http://www.scribd.com/doc/59274810/Hitchens-Christopher-The-Portable-Atheist#page=135*

Ariely, D: *"The honest truth about dishonesty"* Harper 2012

Berghofer, D, Schwartz, G: "The Ethical Leadership Scales " 2008, Trafford Publishing

Blackburn, Simon (2001): *Ethics: A Very Short Introduction.* Extracts from Wikipedia August 2012

http://www.theskillsportal.com/leadership/35-articles/660-leadership-is-about-trust-and-honesty.html

Andrews, A: "The Noticer: Sometimes all a person needs is a little perspective". Thomas Nelson 2011

Bennis, W: "On becoming as leader". Basic Books Fourth edition 2009

Ciulla, J: "What is good leadership". Centre for Public Leadership, Working Paper. Taken from http://dspace.mit.edu/bitstream/handle/1721.1/55929/CPL_WP_04_0 7_Ciulla.pdf?sequence=1 accessed November 2012.

Cloke, K: "Mediating Dangerously. The frontiers of conflict resolution". Jossey-Bass 2001

"Hume, D: The Natural History of Religion." In Hitchens, Christopher (2007). *The Portable Atheist: Essential Readings for the Nonbeliever, Chapter 5. Also accessible over http://www.scribd.com/doc/59274810/Hitchens-Christopher-The-Portable-Atheist#page=33*

Huron Consulting Group: *"The New world of disclosure under Subanes-Oxley" ABI Journey 2003*

Kelly, R: *"The power of Followship" 1992. Extracts accessed via http://changingminds.org/disciplines/leadership/followship/kelley_follo wer.htm*

King, Iian: *"How to Make Good Decisions and Be Right All the Time: Solving the Riddle of Right and Wrong"*, 2009 Extracts from the introduction and Chapter 26. Continuum 2008

Kouzes, J & Poznar, B: "The Truth about leadership". Jersey -Bass 2010

Krogerus, M, Tschäppeler, R: "The decision book. Fifty models for strategic decision making" Profile books 2010

Levitt, T: "Marketing Myopia", Harvard Business Review reprint number 75507, 1975 accessed September 2012 from http://www.casadogalo.com/marketingmyopia.pdf pages 11/12

Miller, Barbara Stoler (2004): *The Bhagavad Gita: Krishna's Counsel in Time of War*. New York: Random House. p. 3. Lifted from Wikipedia August 2012

Narciso, D: "Rolling Uphill: Realizing the honesty of atheism". Aeon Publishing Inc 2004.

Nelson, S & Ortmeier, J: "A guide to great leadership" MDA Leadership consulting 2011

Nyberg, D: "The Varnished Truth". University of Chicago Press 1995

Shalvi, S, Eldar, O, Bereby-Meyer, Y: "When do we lie" Psychological Journal September 4 2012. Extract lifted from The Daily Telegraph, September 7 2012

Shu, L, Gina, F, Bazzerman, M: "Dishonest Deed, Clear Conscience: Self-Preservation through Moral Disengagement and Motivated Forgetting". Harvard Paper 09-078 dated 2009, accessed via http://www.hbs.edu/research/pdf/09-078.pdf

Spencer, S: "The Heart of Leadership. Unlock your inner wisdom and inspire others." section "voicing truth". Rider 2004

Trevino, L, Nelson, K: "Managing Business ethics" chapter 9 page 343 reference to J. Burke study

Warlizard: "8 corporate lies you think are true but aren't" (extract from "How to Steal your bosses job". Warlizard Ink. 2011

WEB SITES & MAGAZINE ARTICLES

Part 1 "Searching for Honesty"

Atheism: http://en.wikipedia.org/wiki/Atheism
accessed August 2012

"Are Americans becoming less religious"
http://www.patheos.com/blogs/friendlyatheist/2009/12/27/gallup-poll-americans-are-becoming-less-religious/
accessed September 2012

Akerlof & Loyalty: http://www.scribd.com/doc/94183339/AKERLOF-Loyalty
accessed August 2012

Bandura, A: (1990). Selective activation and disengagement of moral control. *Journal of Social Issues,* 46, 27-46. & (1999). Moral disengagement in the preparation of inhumanities. *Personal and Social Psychology Review*, 3, 193–209.

Barry, P: "Powerful business leaders, Rupert Murdoch"
http://www.leadingcompany.com.au/leadership/powerful-business-leaders-rupert-murdoch/201206211506
accessed November 2012

BBC study Martin Luther King:
http://www.bbc.co.uk/history/recent/martin_luther_king_01.shtml
accessed October 2012

Beckoff, M: "The ethical dog"
http://www.scientificamerican.com/article.cfm?id=the-ethical-dog&page=2
accessed October 2012

Cablevision: 2009 (extract)
http://consumerist.com/2008/04/cablevision-blatantly-lies-to-subscribers-as-the-fcc-twiddles-its-thumbs.html
accessed September 2012

"Can you be honest, intelligent & religious"?
http://www.patheos.com/blogs/friendlyatheist/2010/05/05/can-you-be-honest-intelligent-and-religious/
accessed September 2012

"Charismatic leadership in a mass struggle" (Martin L. King)
http://mlk-kpp01.stanford.edu/kingweb/additional_resources/articles/charisma.htm
accessed October 2012

Code of Business standards, News Corporation, May 2011
http://www.newscorp.com/PDF/StdBusinessConduct_2011.pdf
accessed August 2012

"Deceitful Minds", Time Magazine Mar 13 2000 (quoting Stiegnitz and C. Lohmann)
http://www.time.com/time/world/article/0,8599,2056196,00.html
accessed September 2012

"Empowerment systems"
http://www.empowermentsystems.com/tp10trth.html
accessed August 2012

Fullan, Michael: "Moral purpose writ large" extracted from
http://www.cdl.org/resource-library/articles/moral_purpose.php
accessed October 2012

Goleman, D: "What makes a Leader" published in Harvard Business
Review 2004. http://hbr.org/2004/01/what-makes-a-leader/ar/1
accessed September 2012

Goleman, D, Boyatzis, R, McKee, A; "Primal Leadership – Then hidden
driver of great performance" Harvard Business Review 2001
http://hbr.org/2001/12/primal-leadership-the-hidden-driver-of-great-
performance/ar/1 and http://www.businesslistening.com/primal-
leadership.php accessed September 2012

"Green, J, Paxton, J: "Patterns of neural activity associated with
honest and dishonest moral decisions" 2009
http://www.wjh.harvard.edu/~jgreene/GreeneWJH/Greene-Paxton-
Honesty-Dishonesty-PNAS09.pdf
accessed September 2012

"Gods honest truth"
http://www.guardian.co.uk/commentisfree/2007/oct/18/godshonesttru
th accessed September 2012

Haidt,H: moral and emotional studies
http://en.wikipedia.org/wiki/Jonathan_Haidt
accessed September 2012

Hartmann, T: "Now corporations have the right to lie"
http://www.commondreams.org/views03/0101-07.htm
accessed September 2012

Hindu ancient text, Mahanharata Santi Parva
http://archive.org/stream/TheMahabharataOfKrishna-
dwaipayanaVyasa/MahabharataOfVyasa-
EnglishTranslationByKMGanguli_djvu.txt

accessed November 2012

Honduran factory worker data (Nike case)
http://en.wikipedia.org/wiki/Sweatshop
accessed September 2012.

"Honesty is the best policy"
http://www.dailymail.co.uk/health/article-2184876/Honesty-best-policy-telling-fewer-lies-improve-physical-mental-health.ht-ml#ixzz24NTWDEZY
accessed August 2012

Huron Consulting Goup 2003 (extract)
http://blog.nbacls.com/2010/01/15/accounting-fraud-and-financial-restatement.aspx
accessed September 2012

Index on Censorship
http://www.mediamonitors.net/mosaddeq32.html#_edn1
quoting John Swainton, Vol. 30, No. 1, January 2001, p. 10.
accessed September 2012

"Is atheism increasing or just honesty about atheism"?
http://atheism.about.com/b/2007/08/20/is-atheism-increasing-or-just-honesty-about-atheism.htm
accessed September 2012

Lehman Brothers case:
http://en.wikipedia.org/wiki/Lehman_Brothers
accessed August 2012

"Lets be honest"
http://truth-saves.com/lets-be-honest/
accessed September 2012

Lies
http://en.wikipedia.org/wiki/Lie
accessed August 2012

"Love my enemy", extracts from Bandura 1990 & 1999
http://www.lovemyenemy.com/moral-disengagement/
accessed September 2012

Mertz, Jon: The Leadership Honesty spectrum, extracted from
http://leadchangegroup.com/are-we-completely-honest-leaders/,

"Morality"
http://en.wikipedia.org/wiki/Morality
for quote on William Damon, accessed August 2012

Nike case California 1998 – 2002
http://www.monitor.net/monitor/0309a/copyright/nikesuitend.html
accessed September 2012

Office depot staff (extract)
http://blog.laptopmag.com/source-office-depot-associates-routinely-lie-about-notebook-stock
accessed September 2012

New York Times, Company ethics 2005
http://www.nytco.com/company-properties-times-coe.html
accessed September 2012

Permissible lying
http://www.jlaw.com/Articles/hf_LyingPermissible.html
accessed September 2012

Rupert Murdoch leadership style
http://www.studymode.com/essays/Rupert-Murdoch-622016.html
accessed November 2012

"Rupert Murdoch – the media mogul"
http://www.icmrindia.org/casestudies/catalogue/Business%20Strategy2/Business%20Strategy%20Rupert%20Murdoch-The%20Media%20Mogul.htm
accessed November 2012

Society of Professional journalists – code of ethical conduct
http://www.spj.org/ethicscode.asp
accessed September 2012

Truth
http://en.wikipedia.org/wiki/Truth
accessed August 2012

"Truth or lies" http://seedmagazine.com/content/article/truth_or_lies/
August 17, 2009, accessed August 2012

"The protestant ethic and spirit of capitalism"
http://en.wikipedia.org/wiki/The_Protestant_Ethic_and_the_Spirit_of_Capitalism

The Bible: New International Version

Weiss, L Ph.D. "What is the emperor wearing"? Truth telling in business relationships" (extracts)

"Why we lie and how we become more honest" The Boston Globe, August 26 2012
http://www.bostonglobe.com/lifestyle/health-wellness/2012/08/26/why-lie-and-how-can-become-more-honest/49WxpXiens6Ark07tyH1jI/story.html

youguv survey for Microsoft 2005
http://www.management-issues.com/2006/8/24/research/corporate-culture-encourages-lying.asp accessed September 2012

"The trolley problem" http://en.wikipedia.org/wiki/Trolley_problem accessed September 2012

Xuetong, Yan; "The problem of mutual trust" International Herald Tribune November 16, 2012

Part II Searching for Leadership

"Character & Traits in Leadership"
http://www.nwlink.com/~donclark/leader/leadchr.html
accessed September 2012

"Ethical leadership – traits"
http://www.managementstudyguide.com/leadership-ethics.htm
accessed October 2012

Importance of ethical leadership, quote by Gael O Brien:
http://freemanblog.freeman.tulane.edu/freemannews/index.php/crisis-experts-tout-importance-of-ethical-leadership/
accessed October 2012

Ethical leadership & remarks of Alan Greenspan 2002 , extracted from http://www.ethicalleadership.com/BusinessArticle.htm accessed October 2012

"Ethics & behaving ethically"
http://www.businessballs.com/ethical_management_leadership.htm
accessed September 2012

Ethical leadership in business: http://highered.mcgraw-hill.com/sites/0073526703/student_view0/ebook/chapter1/chbody1/the_importance_of_ethics_in_business.html
accessed October 2012

Ethical Credo @ Johnson & Johnson:
http://www.jnj.com/responsibility/ESG/Governance/Overview
accessed October 2012

Ethical code of conduct @ Microsoft:
http://www.microsoft.com/about/legal/en/us/Compliance/Buscond/Default.aspx
accessed October 2012

Ethical Leadership example BMW:
http://www.bmw.com/com/en/insights/corporation/sustainability/content.html
accessed October 2012

Ethical Leadership example BP:
http://www.bp.com/extendedsectiongenericarticle.do?categoryId=9039352&contentId=7072114
accessed October 2012

Ethical code of conduct @ Intel:
http://www.intel.com/content/www/us/en/policy/policy-code-conduct-corporate-information.html
accessed October 2012

"Followship", including reasons to and not to follow leaders.
http://changingminds.org/disciplines/leadership/followship/followship.htm
accessed September 2012

Gant, R "An exploration of followship" research paper
http://www.antiochne.edu/om/mba/docs/GallantLeadershipPaperFall2011.pdf
accessed September 2012

Gunn, R, "Am I a Leader"
http://tsp-leadership.pbworks.com/f/AmIaLeader.pdf
accessed September 2012

Iron lady leadership
http://ironladyleadership.wikispaces.com/Leadership+Styles accessed
October 2012

"Is president Obama a good leader?"
http://www.bbc.co.uk/news/world-15567046
accessed November 2012

"Is Obama black enough"?
http://www.time.com/time/nation/article/0,8599,1584736,00.html
accessed November 2012

Thatcher quotes
http://www.igreens.org.uk/margaret_thatcher_quotes.htm accessed
October 2012

Leadership styles (Thatcher)
http://baderalhablani.blogspot.ch/2012/03/leadership-styles-of-
margaret-thatcher.html
accessed October 2012

Kellerman, B. (2007). "*What Every Leader Needs to Know About
Followers*". *Harvard Business Review*, December 2007, pp. 84 – 91

Kelly, R "Followship typologies" – extracts published on
http://ambiguityadvantage.blogspot.ch/2008/06/kellys-typology-of-
followship.html
accessed September 2012

Leadership: http://en.wikipedia.org/wiki/Leadership

Leadership definitions
http://expertscolumn.com/content/great-definitions-leadership
accessed September 2012

Leadership styles
http://www.nwlink.com/~donclark/leader/leadstl.html
accessed September 2012

"Managers or leaders – or both?" (Reference to Hay Group Lamb &
McKee survey 2004)
http://smallbusinessangel.wordpress.com/2009/03/30/what-does-it-
mean-to-be-a-leader/
accessed September 2012

"Obamas style – the new way of leadership?"
http://www.psychologytoday.com/blog/the-intuitive-compass/201110/obamas-leadership-the-new-way-leadership
accessed November 2012

"Obama is President but is he a leader" (quoting D Brooks New York Times):
http://www.outsidethebeltway.com/obama-is-president-but-is-he-a-leader/
accessed November 2012

Schuler, A. J. Dr. "Leadership self test"
http://www.schulersolutions.com/leadership_self_test.html
accessed September 2012 . This was kindly reproduced with permission of Dr. A. J. Schuler, an expert in leadership and Organisational change. To find out more about his programmes and services, visit www.SchulerSolutions.com or call (703) 370-6545.

"The real lessons of Steve Jobs"
http://hbr.org/2012/04/the-real-leadership-lessons-of-steve-jobs/
accessed October 2012

"The Steve Jobs way"
http://www.strategy-business.com/article/00109?gko=d331b accessed October 2012

Trevino, L. K., Brown, M. & Hartman, L. P. (2003): A qualitative investigation of perceived executive ethical leadership: Perceptions from inside and outside the executive suite. Human Relations, 56(1), 5 – 37. Extracted from Wikipedia:
http://en.wikipedia.org/wiki/Ethical_leadership
accessed September 2012

Whipple, B: "The synopsis of trust" referring to Bennis and Jim Burke of Johnson & Johnson
http://leadergrow.com/articles/151-the-synapse-of-trust
accessed September 2012

Williams, R: "Why Steve Jobs was not a leader"
http://www.psychologytoday.com/blog/wired-success/201204/why-steve-jobs-was-not-leader
accessed October 2012

Part III Realising the benefits

BMW Group. Sustainable Value report, 2007/2008. Available over bmw.com

"Apple doctrine", Tom Cook interview 2009, CEO Apple
http://features.blogs.fortune.cnn.com/2009/01/22/the-cook-doctrine-at-apple/
accessed November 2012

"Bad news, but Iluka boss deserves and award for honesty"
http://www.theaustralian.com.au/business/opinion/bad-news-but-iluka-boss-deserves-praise-for-honesty/story-fnciil7d-1226422930223
accessed November 2012

 "Boart Longyear sacks chief"
http://www.leadingcompany.com.au/leadership-styles/boart-longyear-sacks-chief-too-honest-for-his-own-good/201210042671
accessed November 2012

BP profile: Brand Directory.com
accessed November 2012

"Carlos Ghosn – The turnaround specialist"
http://www.icmrindia.org/casestudies/catalogue/Leadership%20and%20Entrepreneurship/Carlos%20Ghosn-The%20Turnaround%20Specialist-Leadership%20and%20Entrepreneurship-Case%20Studies.htm#Management_and_Leadership_Style accessed November 2012

Carlos Ghosn: Interview with CNN 2005:
http://edition.cnn.com/2005/BUSINESS/04/20/boardroom.ghosn/
accessed November 2012

BCIPD (Chartered Institute of Personnel & Development) "Employee engagement and well-being"
http://www.hi-mag.com/health-insurance/product-area/occupational-health/article403762.ece
accessed November 2012

CIPD Employee engagement survey Summer 2012
http://www.cipd.co.uk/binaries/5923 Employee Outlook SR (WEB).pdf
accessed November 2012

CIMA "Corporate reputation: perspectives of measuring and managing principle risk" June 2007.
http://www.cimaglobal.com/Documents/Thought_leadership_docs/cid_exrep_corporate_reputation_june07.pdf
accessed November 2012

Covey, S: "How the best leaders build trust"
http://www.leadershipnow.com/CoveyOnTrust.html
accessed December 2012

Dawkins, J (2004): "Corporate responsibility: the communication challenge" in *Journal of Communications Management*,
Volume 9, Issue 3
accessed November 2012

DDI (Development Dimensions International) "Trust in the workplace"
http://www.ddiworld.com/DDIWorld/media/white-papers/trustmonograph_mg_ddi.pdf?ext=.pdf
accessed November 2012

Dean, A, Sobel, R: "Has Wal-Mart buried mom & pop": analysis of the impact of Wal-Mart on Small business spring 2008:
http://www.cato.org/pubs/regulation/regv31n1/v31n1-1.pdf
accessed November 2012

Employee Engagement survey 2011 – Blessing White
http://www.blessingwhite.com/content/reports/blessingwhite_2011_ee_report.pdf
accessed November 2012

"Employees do not trust their leaders" extracts from Maritz research 2010 http://www.greatleadershipbydan.com/2010/04/new-poll-employees-dont-trust-their.html
accessed November 2012

Fortune 500 company financial data:
http://money.cnn.com/magazines/fortune/fortune500/2011/full_list/
accessed November 2012

Harrison, K: "Corporate reputation" quoting Charles Fombrun
http://www.cuttingedgepr.com/articles/corprep_important.asp
accessed November 2012

"Honest Commmnication on Business benefits :corporate social responsibility". Parker Wayne & kent.
http://www.pwkpr.com/downloads/corporate_social_responsibility_public_relations.pdf
accessed November 2012

Intel Mission and Vision & corporate sustainability reports
www.intel.com
accessed November 2012

"Johnson & Johnson"
www.jnj.com
accessed November 2012

Kenexa: "Trust Matters – New links to employee retention and well-being": 2011/2012
http://khpi.com/documents/KHPI-WorkTrends-Report-Trust-Matters
accessed November 2012

"Leadership style and employee well being"
http://www.psychologytoday.com/blog/the-good-life/200809/leadership-style-and-employee-well-being
accessed November 2012

Leadership style of Richard Branson
http://michael.walenius.com/?p=141
accessed October 2012

 "Linking strong moral principles to business success" Moral Intelligence
http://knowledge.wharton.upenn.edu/article.cfm?articleid=1264
quoting *Moral Intelligence: Enhancing Business Performance & Leadership Success* (Wharton School Publishing), 2005
accessed November 2012

"Lighting the path to success" The Worlds most Admired companies, Hay Group & Fortune. April 2012
http://www.haygroup.com/fortune/downloads/2012-FORTUNE-Lighting-the-path-to-success.pdf
accessed November 2012

Lopez, V, Garcia, A, Rodriguez, L: "Sustainable development and corporate performance. A study based on the Dow Jones sustainability Index, 2007.
http://link.springer.com/article/10.1007%2Fs10551-006-9253-8?LI=true#page-1
accessed November 2012

Maritz Institute White Paper 2011 "The Human Science of giving recognition"
http://www.maritz.com/~/media/Files/MaritzDotCom/White Papers/Motivation/White_Paper_The_Science_of_Giving_Recognition1.ashx
accessed November 2012

Maritz Institute Employee Values study
http://www.maritz.com/Employee-Values-Study.aspx
accessed November 2012

Mourkogiannis, Nikos "The realists guide to moral purpose". Published in Strategy & Business Winter 2005 Issue 41, extracted from
http://www.strategy-business.com/article/05405?pg=all
accessed October 2012

Nestlé company overview
www.Nestlé.com
accessed November 2012

Nestlé Insider overview
http://www.vault.com/wps/portal/usa/companies/company-profile/Nestlé-SA?companyId=55007
accessed November 2012

New York Times June 25 2000 "Tough jeans, a soft heart and frayed earnings at Levis Strauss" accessed from
http://karlschoenberger.com/LeviNYT.html
accessed November 2012

Quotes, Richard Branson
http://www.evancarmichael.com/Famous-Entrepreneurs/592/Richard-Branson-Quotes.html
accessed October 2012

Rupert Murdoch
http://www.biography.com/people/rupert-murdoch-9418489?page=3
accessed November 2012

Schwaiger, M "Components and Parameters of Corporate reputation",
parts 1 – 4 from the Schmalenbach Business Review, January 2004
http://www.sbr-online.de/pdfarchive/einzelne_pdf/sbr_2004_jan-046-
071.pdf
accessed November 2012

Social responsibility@BP
http://www.bp.com/sectionbodycopy.do?categoryId=3311&contentId=
7066754
accessed November 2012

Stephenson, C "Rebuilding trust: The integral role of leadership in
fostering values, honesty and vision"
http://www.iveybusinessjournal.com/departments/from-the-
dean/rebuilding-trust-the-integral-role-of-leadership-in-fostering-
values-honesty-and-vision
accessed December 2012

Suen, W: "Alliance strategy and the fall of Swissair"
http://www.scribd.com/doc/48784159/Alliance-strategy-and-the-fall-
of-Swissair
accessed November 2012

TalentKeepers research 2004 "Trust linked to employee retention"
http://www.prweb.com/releases/2004/03/prweb113268.htm
accessed November 2012

Toyota Overview
www.toyota-global.com
accessed November 2012

Toyota finances and overview
www.yahoofinance.com
accessed November 2012

Toyota stock price dilemmas CBS news quote:
http://www.cbsnews.com/2100-500395_162-6320021.html accessed
November 2012

"Tylenol and the legacy of J&J´s James Burke"
http://business.time.com/2012/10/05/tylenol-and-the-legacy-of-jjs-james-burke
accessed November 2012

The Tylenol Crisis
http://iml.jou.ufl.edu/projects/fall02/susi/tylenol.htm
accessed November 2012

UBS cuts 10,000 employees, interview with Sergio Ermotti CEO
"Twenty minutes online" 31 October 2012

UBS Corporate strategy
http://www.ubs.com/global/en/about_ubs/about_us/strategy.html
accessed November 2012

UBS annual report 2011
www.UBS.com
accessed November 2012

WP Carey school conference extract with PepsiCo CEO Craig
Weatherup "whats your leadership model"
http://knowwpcarey.com/article.cfm?aid=59
accessed November 2012

Part IV Finding the answers

Institute for ethical leadership: "The ethical leadership scales":
http://www.ethicalleadership.com/EthicalLeadershipScales.html
accessed November 2012

Myatt, M: "Communication tips of great leaders"
http://www.forbes.com/sites/mikemyatt/2012/04/04/10-communication-secrets-of-great-leaders/
accessed November 2012

Index

www.ingramcontent.com/pod-product-compliance
Lightning Source LLC
Chambersburg PA
CBHW060008210326
41520CB00009B/859